Another Long Hot Soak

BOOK TWO

Over 50 Stories to
Warm the Heart
and Inspire the Spirit

Edited by **Chris Gidney**
INTRODUCED BY WENDY CRAIG

ZONDERVAN™

GRAND RAPIDS, MICHIGAN 49530 USA

We want to hear from you. Please send your comments about this book to us in care of the address below. Thank you.

ZONDERVAN™

Another Long Hot Soak – Book Two
Copyright © 2002 by Chris Gidney and Guideposts, Carmel, New York 10512

Requests for information should be addressed to:

Zondervan, *Grand Rapids, Michigan 49530*

The author asserts the moral right to be identified as the compiler of this work.

ISBN 0-310-25176-1

Printed in the United States

05 06 07 08 /❖DC/ 10 9 8 7 6

CONTENTS

3. When Hope is Restored

4. When Loneliness is Conquered

5. When Faith Holds On

FOREWORD

by Chris Gidney

Isn't it amazing how much time we spend looking after ourselves? We join leisure clubs, eat health food, experience therapy, jog round the block, endure medical tests, visit our dentist regularly, and take vitamin pills. However, most of us are aware that we are not just mind and body, but spirit too. Yet how much time do we spend looking after our spiritual side? Why do we invest so much time and energy into our bodies but ignore the soul? These true stories, anecdotes and poems express the real thoughts and experiences of those who have found consideration of their spiritual life important. No amount of jogging will help you overcome fear, but solutions to this and many other of life's hurdles can be found by exploring your 'inner' self, the very deepest part of you, created and placed there by God himself.

INTRODUCTION
by Wendy Craig

Award winning actress and writer Wendy Craig is everybody's favourite TV 'Mum'. Starring for more than twelve years in such television series as 'Not in Front of the Children'; 'And Mother Makes Three'; 'And Mother Makes Five' as well as the much acclaimed 'Butterflies', these BBC classics are now being shown on Sky TV for a new generation to enjoy.

Wendy's list of awards give an idea of the amount of love and esteem in which she is held in and out of her profession. Having been Actress of the Year, BBC Personality of the Year, as well as BBC TV's Woman of the Year, it is no great surprise to know that she was also voted The Funniest Woman on Television.

Yet for all this accolade, it would be difficult to find a more unassuming actress, possibly because Wendy is aware of her own fallibility and needs. She is the widow of musician and journalist Jack Bentley after being married for thirty-nine years. She has two sons, Alaster, an oboist with the Birmingham Royal Ballet, and Ross, a writer.

Life is often more akin to a Blackpool roller coaster than the calm, serene and pleasant life that we would all wish for. Talents, knowledge, money, family, friends and even self confidence seem unable to change the course of our lives. As Tom Hank's character in the film *Forest Gump* said, 'Life is like a box of chocolates. You never know what you're going to get!'

In common with a lot of actors, I am not the most confident person in the world. I am so often filled with doubt, doubt of every kind, including self-doubt. Many times I have stood in the wings at the side of the stage before making my entrance, filled with terror and convinced that I'd never get through the show. I've often sensed my own inadequacy and felt my confidence ebbing away, and I'm sure this must sound impossible to those who see me exuding confidence and energy when I'm on the television or stage, but this is the truth.

In the midst of the gloomier parts of life, isn't it a wonderful thing when someone shares a story of how they overcame their own particular difficulty. Suddenly the impossible seems reachable, the dark clouds of despair move to reveal a bright rainbow of colour, and life is in perspective once more.

Another Long Hot Soak contains the true stories of those who found that they had the ability to overcome whatever life threw at them. Minor details and some names have been changed in order to protect the privacy of the individuals concerned, but they all discovered they could triumph over the trials and tribulations through an inner strength they never knew existed. Many acknowledge a power bigger than themselves which ultimately gave them the strength to cope.

Facing serious illness or imminent death, nightmare scenarios of being lost in a jungle and the deep pain of a relationship that went wrong, these are just some of the experiences contained within. Most of these stories are new to me, but they all contain an essential ingredient which I have discovered to be vital in my own life: faith and hope.

Whether you are on the 'downward' slide of the roller coaster, or on the 'climb to the top', I am sure these stories will provide inspiration, encouragement and a source of hope that will enable you to find the 'handle' to steady you through the dips and bumps of your own journey on life's great adventures.

1

WHEN LOVE
BREAKS THROUGH

Nothing can transform one's life
so dramatically as love breaking through.
It is like the sun bursting through dark clouds.
Suddenly everything is amazingly different.

Wendy Craig

SEVEN WORDS THAT CHANGED MY LIFE

by Mary Bird

A simple whisper shows a small girl she is loved.

I grew up knowing I was different. I was born with a cleft palate, and when I started to go to school, my classmates – who were constantly teasing – made it clear to me how I must look to others: a little girl with a misshapen lip, crooked nose, lopsided teeth, and hollow and somewhat garbled speech. I couldn't even blow up a balloon without holding my nose, and when I bent to drink from a fountain, the water spilled out of my nose.

When schoolmates asked 'What happened to your lip?' I'd tell them that I had fallen as a baby and cut it on a piece of glass. Somehow it seemed more acceptable to have suffered an accident than to have been born different. By the age of seven I was convinced that no one outside my own family could ever love me – or even like me.

And then I entered second grade and Mrs Leonard's class.

I never knew what her first name was, just Mrs Leonard. She was round and pretty and fragrant, with chubby arms and shiny brown hair, and warm dark eyes that smiled even on the rare occasions when her mouth didn't. Everyone adored her. But no one came to love her more than I did. And for a special reason.

The time came for the annual hearing tests given at our school. I was barely able to hear anything out of one ear, and was not about to reveal yet another problem that would single me out as different. And so I cheated. I had learned to watch the other children and raise my hand when they did during group testing. The 'whisper test', however, required a different kind of deception. Each child would go to the door of the classroom, turn sideways, close one ear with a finger, and the teacher would whisper something from her desk, which the child would repeat. Then the same thing was done for the other ear. I had discovered in primary school that nobody checked to see how tightly the untested ear was being covered, so I merely pretended to block mine.

As usual, I was last, but all through the testing I wondered what Mrs Leonard might say to me. I knew from previous years that the teacher whispered things like 'The sky is blue' or 'Do you have new shoes?'

My turn came. I turned my bad ear to her, plugging up the other solidly with my finger, then gently backed my finger out enough to be able to hear. I waited, and then came the words that God had surely put into her mouth. Seven words that changed my life forever.

Mrs Leonard, the pretty, fragrant teacher I adored, said softly, 'I wish you were my little girl.'

LOVE GOES FURTHER
by Bob Considine

A broken relationship is wonderfully restored.

This is the story of a woman's love for her husband. Whether he deserved that love – and why he acted the way he did – are questions I can't answer. I'm not going to write about Karl Taylor; this story is about his wife.

The story begins early in 1950 in the Taylors' small flat. Edith Taylor was sure that she was the 'happiest woman alive'. She and Karl had been married twenty-three years, and her heart still skipped a beat when he walked into the room.

As for Karl, he gave every appearance of a man in love with his wife. Indeed, he seemed almost dependent on her, as if he didn't want to be gone too long away from her. If his job as a government warehouse worker took him out of town, he'd write Edith a long letter every night and drop her postcards several times during the day. He sent small gifts from every place he visited.

Often at night they'd sit up late in their flat and talk about the house they'd own someday, 'when we can make the down-payment'.

In February, 1950, the government sent Karl to Okinawa for a few months to work in a new warehouse. It was a long time to be away – and so far!

This time no little gifts came. Edith understood. He was putting every penny he saved into the bank for their home. Hadn't she begged him for years not to spend so much on her, to save it for the house?

The lonesome months dragged on, and it seemed to Edith that the job over there was taking longer and longer. Each time she expected him home he'd write that he must stay 'another three weeks', 'another month', 'just two months longer'.

He had been gone a year now – and suddenly Edith had an inspiration. Why not buy their home now, before Karl got back, as a surprise for him! She was working now and putting all her earnings in the bank. So she made a down-payment on a cosy cottage with lots of trees and a view.

Karl's letters were coming less and less often. No gifts she understood. But a few pennies for a postage stamp?

Then, after weeks of silence, came a letter:

'Dear Edith. I wish there were a kinder way to tell you that we are no longer married …'

Edith walked to the sofa and sat down. He had arranged a divorce.

The woman lived on Okinawa. She was Japanese; Aiko, maid-of-all-work assigned to clean his room. She was nineteen.

Edith was forty-eight.

Now, if I were making up this story, the rejected wife would feel first shock, then fury. She would fight that quick paper-divorce; she would hate her husband and the woman. She would want vengeance for her own shattered life.

But what I am describing here simply is not what happened. Edith Taylor did not hate Karl. Perhaps she had loved him so long she was unable to stop loving him.

She could picture the situation so well. A penniless girl. A lonely man who – Edith knew it – sometimes drank more than he should. Constant closeness. But even so (here Edith made an heroic effort to be proud of her husband) – even so, Karl had not done the easy, shameful thing. He had chosen the hard way of divorce, rather than take advantage of a young servant-girl.

The only thing Edith could not believe was that he had stopped loving her. That he loved Aiko, too, she made herself accept.

But the difference in their ages, in their backgrounds – this couldn't be the kind of love she and Karl had known! Someday they would both discover this – someday, somehow, Karl would come home.

Edith now built her life around this thought. She wrote to Karl, asking him to keep her in touch with the small, day-to-day things in his life. She sold the little cottage with its view. Karl never knew about it.

He wrote one day that he and Aiko were expecting a baby. Marie was born in 1951, then in 1953, Helen. Edith sent gifts to the little girls. She still wrote to Karl and he wrote back, the comfortable letters of two people who knew each other very well: Helen had a tooth, Aiko's English was improving, Karl had lost weight.

Edith's life was lived now on Okinawa. She merely went through the motions of existence at her flat. Back and forth between factory and home, her mind was always on Karl. Someday he'll come back...

And then the terrible letter: Karl was dying of lung cancer.

Karl's last letters were filled with fear. Not for himself, but for Aiko, and especially for his two little girls. He had been saving to send them to school in America, but his hospital bills were taking everything. What would become of them?

Then Edith knew that her last gift to Karl could be peace of mind for these final weeks. She wrote to him that, if Aiko were willing, she would take Marie and Helen and bring them up in her own home.

For many months after Karl's death, Aiko would not let the children go. They were all she had ever known. Yet what could she offer them except a life like hers had been? A life of poverty, servitude and despair. In November, 1956, she sent the girls to her 'dear Aunt Edith'.

Edith had known it would be hard to be mother at fifty-four to a three-year-old and a five-year-old. She hadn't known that in the time since Karl's death they would forget the little English they knew.

But Marie and Helen learned fast. The fear left their eyes, their faces grew plump. And Edith – for the first time in six years – was hurrying home from work. Even getting meals was fun again!

Sadder were the times when letters came from Aiko. 'Aunt. Tell me now what they do. If Marie or Helen cry or not.' In the broken English Edith read the loneliness, and she knew what loneliness was.

Money was another problem. Edith hired a woman to care for the girls while she worked. Being both mother and wage-earner left her thin and tired. In February she became ill, but she kept working because she was afraid to lose a day's pay; at the factory one day she fainted. She was in the hospital two weeks with pneumonia.

There in the hospital bed, she faced the fact that she would be old before the girls were grown. She thought she had done everything that love for Karl asked of her, but now she knew there was one thing more. She must bring the girls' real mother here too.

She had made the decision, but doing it was something else. Aiko was still a Japanese citizen, and that immigration quota had a waiting list many years long.

It was then that Edith Taylor wrote to me, telling me her story and asking if I could help her. I described the situation in my newspaper column. Others did more. Petitions were started, a special bill speeded through and, in August, 1957, Aiko Taylor was permitted to enter the country.

As the plane came in at the airport, Edith had a moment of fear. What if she should hate this woman who had taken Karl away from her?

The last person off the plane was a girl so thin and small Edith thought at first it was a child. She did not come down the stairs, she only stood there, clutching the railing, and Edith knew that, if she had been afraid, Aiko was near panic.

She called Aiko's name and the girl rushed down the steps and into Edith's arms. In that brief moment, as they held each other, Edith had an extraordinary thought. 'Help me to love this girl, as if she were part of Karl, come home. I prayed for him to come back.

18

Now he was in his two little daughters and in this gentle girl that he loved. Help me, God, to know that.'

Edith's prayers have been answered. Today – seven years after this story took place, Edith and Aiko Taylor and the two growing girls live together in the flat. 'Aunt Edith' is the proud 'other mother' to Aiko's children. Marie, who was confirmed recently, is doing really well at school. Helen has been found to have a talent for ballet and has been accepted by a ballet school. Aiko now speaks fluent English and plans to visit her family in Japan. Edith writes that though 'God has taken one life I loved dearly, He has given me three others to love. I am so thankful.'

A THING OF BEAUTY

by Kenneth Lynch

The chalice that changed a life.

Years ago, I had a jeweller's shop on the west side of the city. One day an elderly woman came in. When she asked if we could make a chalice for her, I was ready to shake my head.

In the first place, judging from her threadbare coat and her work-gnarled hands, I felt sure she couldn't afford such a costly piece. Such works, as used in serving Holy Communion in churches, are usually hand-crafted out of silver and plated with gold. And I didn't have the heart to tell her how much one would cost.

But then, the Gaelic lilt in her voice reminded me of my own great aunts from Ireland. And when she explained that as the mother of a large family, now all grown and dispersed, she wanted the chalice as a gift for her youngest son, shortly to be ordained as a priest, my heart melted. 'How much....' she ventured. 'How much would you say such a thing would cost?' Reaching inside her coat, she withdrew a roll of worn notes. 'I've saved through the years for this,' she said, lifting her chin a bit, 'and I have forty-three pounds. Will it be enough?'

I was in a dilemma. The bottom price for a hand-wrought chalice in those days exceeded seventy-five pounds. But she was so hopeful. 'We can do it for thirty-three pounds,' I said.

Her eyes lit up and she pressed the wad of notes into my hand. 'Take it all,' she said 'and make it twice as good. Nothing will be too fine for my youngest on his great day!'

As she walked out of the shop, I turned to see one of our silver-smiths who had been standing in the back watching us. The man was a fine craftsman, and had learnt his art in France. When he worked he was superb, but he couldn't stay away from the bottle. Things had come to a point that I knew I was going to have to let him go, but now, seeing him, I had a strange feeling that I must give him this one last job.

Calling him up, I told him what the woman wanted and in a meaningful way added, 'Now do the best you can.' As he nodded and went to his bench, I prayed that he'd stick to his work and have the chalice ready in time. The silversmith worked hard on it, often until late at night. There were no more days when he'd phone in 'sick' or be in such poor control of himself that I couldn't trust him to forge a hinge. I was surprised at the change in him, and when I'd compliment him on the job he was doing, he'd only give a quick nod and go on with his work.

The chalice was finished on time, and the silversmith brought it to me for my approval. He stood before me straight and proud. His eyes were clear and forthright as he held up the cup, beautifully wrought in gold-plated silver.

'Well done!' I said enthusiastically. 'Well done.'

He then went out and bought a handsome case of polished walnut. He lined it himself with fine deep blue velvet and placed the chalice inside.

When the old woman returned, I presented her with the case. She lifted the lid and fell back and gasped. 'Oh … oh, this is so beautiful … so beautiful!' Then she looked up questioningly. 'Are you sure, Mr Lynch, that forty-three pounds is enough?'

'Of course,' I said, patting her shoulder. And I meant it. She left the shop repeatedly thanking the heavens.

Unfortunately, the silversmith wasn't in the shop at the time, but when he came in later, I told him how pleased she had been. 'That was a wonderful thing you did,' I said, taking his hand. 'You made a woman very, very happy.'

He looked at me for a moment. 'It was something I had to do, Mr Lynch,' he said finally. 'You see, that woman – she is my mother.'

'But why didn't you – ?'

'I've thrown my life away, Mr Lynch. You know that as well as I do. When I was a boy I ran away to sea. Never once did I write home. Now I didn't want my mother to see the drunk her son has become. It's better this way … until I can be sure of myself.'

The next day the silversmith quietly packed his few belongings and left the shop. I never saw him again. But I feel in my heart that he went on to do well. For the mother's love for one of her sons touched the life of another in a way she could have never imagined.

THE DREAM

by Joe Mendez

Looking for success, a man finds something more.

There are some unforgettable dreams so strange or so beautiful you find them difficult to share with others. But one dream I must tell about, for I believe it was from God.

Some years ago, I dreamed I was a famous musician. A young reporter had come to interview me. She was beautiful, with lustrous auburn hair and warm, friendly eyes with crinkly laugh lines. I awoke with my heart pounding. Though I doubted I would ever be famous, I felt certain that God had shown me the woman I would marry. I called her my Dream Princess. Marriage, however, seemed distant. Even though I was thirty-nine, I still hadn't made much of my life.

My ambition was to become a published writer. I had written stories, plays, poems and books, but none had seen print. To support myself, I worked for an auto dealership, washing and selling cars. In my spare time I refereed at school athletic events, and Mum encouraged me: 'Keep your faith, and when you feel hopeless, remember Psalms Twenty-three and Twenty-seven.' Because I firmly believed the promise that God would guide me, I decided to move to the city. That's where the publishers are. Friends and most of my nine brothers and sisters ridiculed me. 'You need contacts, Joe,' warned one. 'The city will eat you up,' said another, laughing. 'You'll be glad to come back home.'

My answer was to buy a one-way ticket. I boarded the train after saying good-bye to my sister, brother-in-law and nephew. One of my two suitcases held all the books, stories, plays and poems I had written, along with four hundred dollars. When I arrived at the Central Station, I set down my suitcases to check the hotel address. When I leaned over to pick them up, the one with my manuscripts and money was gone! Astonished and dumbfounded, I found a policeman. All he could recommend was to file a report. 'Welcome to the city!' someone said, snickering. All I had left was one hundred dollars in my wallet. I checked into a hotel and started looking for work. A few days later, on an evening stroll, I was mugged. I lost my cash and ID. I couldn't believe it. Twice in one week! 'You gotta be careful,' advised the hotel clerk, shrugging his shoulders.

Meanwhile, no publisher was hiring. I searched for any kind of job, but it seemed hopeless. I felt I was at least becoming street-wise, until I went to the rest room in Central Station. Once again I was mugged. This time I was slammed against the wall, and a shiny blade was pressed against my stomach before my assailant fled. Penniless, I went to the Social Security offices. They advised me to call my family. No way, I vowed. I couldn't face the 'I told you so's.' With no place to live, I joined the city's homeless and hungry. The aroma wafting from restaurants tied my stomach in knots. I stared hungrily at half-eaten food in street-corner trash baskets.

Someone said that the Church of St Agnes near Central Station had a drop-in centre where some four hundred people gathered to eat every night. I felt fortunate to join them, but I didn't feel right sleeping there. It was still summer, so I slept in doorways and on park benches. Sometimes I rode the underground or walked the streets all night. I soon learned to wrap myself in newspapers and lie on top of cardboard to stave off the night chill. But finding a job without a home address or identification was hopeless. That was the worst of it – feeling useless, not having anywhere to be, getting awakened by footsteps of lucky people hurrying to work.

Sometimes I thought of my Dream Princess, but now she too seemed a fading illusion. Desolate days blended into a grey emptiness. Some evenings found me in an all-night McDonald's, writing my thoughts in a notebook. Occasionally the manager let me sleep in the closed-off section upstairs.

Autumn was coming, and despite the crowd, I felt alone. Sick at heart, I looked up into the murky sky and wondered if God had forgotten me. I thought of the psalms Mum had me memorise, in which the psalmist continually expressed his faith even in the grimmest of circumstances. Leaning against an iron fence, I sighed: 'Thank you Lord, thank you for taking care of me today. Thank you for what you are going to do for me tomorrow. For whatever comes into my life, I thank you.'

Within a few days I was assigned a bed two nights a week in a local shelter. As I signed in at the table, a young woman walked in from the kitchen. I looked up and my heart skipped a beat. There was my Dream Princess! I stared at her lustrous auburn hair. She had friendly eyes and there was a glow about her face as she walked across the room. My hands trembled and I began composing a love song in my mind.

Haltingly I struck up a conversation. Her name was Carol Ann Perkins. She was a volunteer worker in her mid-forties. She was polite and we talked a bit about my writing aspirations; then she left. But before she was out the door I had finished her song in my mind. A few days later I went to another shelter, at the Methodist Church, where I had come to know the pastor, the Reverend Austin Armitstead. He gave me a typewriter and I typed out the song about my Dream Princess.

Meeting Carol Ann sparked a positive change in my life. I found a part-time job refereeing high school and college athletic events. My self-confidence grew. Three weeks after meeting Carol Ann, I was again a guest at the shelter where she was a volunteer. Having saved a little money, I asked her out to lunch. For a moment I was afraid she was going to turn me down. Then, smiling, she hesitantly said yes. We went to a cafe and over hamburgers fell into easy conversation. I could see there was hurt in her eyes, and I cautiously drew her out. She said she had just ended a relationship with someone and then quickly changed the subject. We parted as friends, but that was all.

Even so, I excitedly phoned my mother about finding my Dream Princess. She said she would pray for her. I asked Carol Ann out again, and this time I brought her a single red rose. For the next four months our relationship continued over lunches, but always on a casual, friendly basis, and obviously not going anywhere. I, of course, was head over heels in love but didn't want to push myself. 'Oh, God,' I prayed, 'this is the girl you showed me in my dream, but she doesn't seem interested in me at all. What should I do?' It turned out I didn't have to do anything. A few days later I discovered a new Carol Ann. I sensed a special warmth in her green eyes, and when she placed her hand on mine as we talked, I was ecstatic.

Later I learned that a friend of hers was making a pilgrimage and Carol Ann had given her a prayer petition to take, asking for 'someone who is kind and gentle, good and loving and only has eyes for me'. It was then she realised that the one courting her was all of those things.

On 12 February 1992, I got down on one knee and with a red rose in hand asked Carol Ann to marry me. Our wedding was offi- ciated by Pastor Armitstead. A friend, Frank Scafuri, sang 'Dreamer, I Wanna Be With You', the song he and I composed from the words I wrote after I first saw Carol Ann. Since then we have made beautiful music together, and every week my Dream Princess still receives a single red rose from me. Carol Ann and I are both work- ing and we volunteer at the two church shelters where I once slept.

Every so often someone down and out looks at me with pain- filled eyes and asks, 'How can you possibly understand what I'm going through?' I sit down with him, put my arm around his shoulders and explain I know exactly what he's going through. I tell him God gives each of us a dream. And if we follow His will, pray and hold on to our faith even through the darkest times, our dreams will come true. Then I tell him about Carol Ann.

THE PARTY

by Lynne Hart

A wife throws a party for a man she wasn't even talking to.

'Pleeeez, let's talk,' I begged for the umpteenth time.

'Get out of my sight,' he snapped, and stormed out of the kitchen.

The now-familiar lump tightened in my throat. Teary-eyed, I dropped into a kitchen chair, crying, 'What's happening to us?' How proud I had been when Mark quit drinking! How perfect life was going to be. Now I laughed at my simple-minded optimism, my great expectations. Alcohol had been Mark's best friend; when he was forced to quit drinking he'd sunk into a stony, severe depression. For six months he'd refused to speak, walking past me as if I were invisible; at most, he'd snarl 'Get lost' or 'Go away'. After twenty-one years of marriage, we were headed for divorce.

That night, I buried my head under the covers, pleading, 'Someone help me!' I wanted to sleep forever. Morning found me worn and weary. Before, I'd always prayed for wisdom, insight and healing, but this morning I cried out in full helplessness: 'Lord, please show me what to do – I don't want this marriage to end!' As I went through my Bible, one verse leapt out from the page 'In this way you shall set the fiftieth year apart and proclaim freedom to all the inhabitants of the land.' It was to be called the 'jubilee' year. That Scripture haunted me all day. Mark's fiftieth birthday was only three weeks away. Was God telling me I should honour his fiftieth year? And if so, in what way? Maybe a birthday party. No, that would be ridiculous. How could I throw Mark a party? We weren't even speaking.

A week passed and that Bible verse still sat in my mind. Even the crazy idea of a party. Finally I thought, *Okay, invite our friends Jane and George for lunch on the Sunday before Mark's birthday. After all, fifty years of life is special.* I called, half-hoping they couldn't make it, but Jane accepted. 'It's a surprise,' I said just before hanging up. I couldn't believe I'd done it.

Four days before the lunch, Mark and I sat on the patio, each pretending to be alone. After weeks of near-total silence, a tense conversation started. Before long it had blazed into an argument. Through gritted teeth Mark snarled, 'This isn't working anymore; I want out,' and he left.

'Get out, then,' I hissed at his departing back. Alone with my whirling thoughts, I cried, 'Lord, how wrong I was! You didn't want a jubilee; I just imagined it. I'm sorry, but I hate him.' *What a foolish idea, planning a party under circumstances like these. It was like arranging deck chairs on the* Titanic. *I'm calling Jane to cancel,* I thought. *I want out too.*

Just then Mark came back. He must have felt bad, for he said in a surprisingly casual tone, 'We have such nice neighbours. It's too bad they haven't been over more often.' Suddenly, my depression lifted and my spirit soared as a voice sounded inside: Jubilee – a celebration! I held my breath. I wanted to laugh, or shout. Instead, I jumped out of my deck chair and into the house to make phone calls – not to cancel the lunch, but to invite all our other neighbours and friends! Amazingly, all the people I called said they'd be delighted to come and offered to bring something. I happily accepted.

Next afternoon, as I stood contemplating an unmade bed, I overheard Mark on the phone with our family doctor. He had badly pulled a muscle in his back. The prescription was hot, half-hour-long baths, four times a day. What a fix! Now I had thirty-two people coming for a surprise party, and I had a dirty house and a bedridden husband who 'wanted out' – yet somehow I knew everything would be fine. I can't explain how, but I knew that this party was the right thing to do. Was I crazy, doing all this for a man who wouldn't speak to me? No, for the first time in my life I felt mysteriously, truly inspired. That night, I slept like a baby, certain I was doing what God wanted me to do.

Saturday, the day before the party, I wanted to make Mark's favourite potato salad. I boiled a party-size pot of potatoes without his noticing. But where would I cool them? I put them in a grocery bag and hid them in the pedal bin. A stroke of genius! When Mark took his next therapeutic bath, I retrieved my potatoes, made the world's fastest potato salad, and hid it safely, way in the back of the refrigerator. A little later our former neighbours, the Bakers, phoned. They'd be in town for a three-day convention – could their daughter, Nancy (our fifteen-year-old daughter Trish's friend), stay with us? The last thing I needed was an overnight guest, but on second thought it gave me the perfect excuse for some frantic housecleaning. Trish, who was in on my plans, whirled into action, scrubbing and dusting and vacuuming and polishing.

By this time I was in a trance. Floating out the door towards the supermarket, I saw a party-supply shop. Decorations! I had almost forgotten! I bought balloons, crepe-paper streamers, a Happy 50th Birthday banner, matching plates and napkins, and lots of candles. While Mark soaked, I hid in the guest room and inflated twenty-five balloons. It was a blessing he was ignoring me, or he might have wondered why my face was blue. All day long Trish sneaked to and from my neighbour Jane's, carrying ground meat, cheese, pickles, hamburger buns, ice cream. 'Take this to Jane's,' I barked like a drill sergeant. 'Buy this! Borrow that from Jane.'

Sunday! Party day was here! Everything was all set, except how to get Mark out of the house. The guests were coming at six. I frantically prayed for a solution. Trish's boyfriend, Eric, called, asking if I needed help. I told him about getting Mark away from the house. 'I'll take care of it,' Eric said. At 5.20 p.m. the Bakers arrived, depositing Nancy and her luggage. Still no word from Eric. What did he have planned? By 5.30 my stomach was churning at high speed. At 5.35 the phone rang and I jumped, spilling my iced tea.

'Hi, Lynne. Is Mark there? It's Jim.' Eric's father! So that's who Eric had enlisted! 'Mark, telephone!' I called, with a silent thank you. Mark fell for Jim's crazy story – that he needed a lift home – and made a quick exit. When he left, I resumed my sergeant's role: 'Hang the balloons and crepe streamers! Hang the birthday banner! Bring all the chairs from the basement!' Jane hurried in through the kitchen with the food.

At six o'clock sharp, in came the guests, carrying beautiful salads, pies, cakes. Instantly, my picnic table was a marvellous crammed display suitable for the cover of *Homes and Gardens*. Trish had baked a big lovely birthday cake at Jane's. With its few errors camouflaged by fifty strategically placed candles, the cake had a warmth and charm that only youth could create. It was the perfect centrepiece. 'We're ready,' I breathed – just as our sentry shouted, 'He's here!' Everyone hurried to the front door, and as Mark entered, we shouted 'SURPRISE!' He gazed in astonishment at the people and at the brightly decorated rooms, and staggered backward against the door. 'You got me!' he exclaimed. 'You really got me!'

Mark stood leaning against the door, totally shocked. Running to him, Trish gave him a big kiss, saying, 'Happy birthday, Daddy!' I followed, kissing him and squeaking, through the catch in my throat, 'Happy birthday, dear.' After eating, and before opening his presents, Mark asked for our attention. He thanked God for Trish and me, for helping us stick together through the tough times, and for such wonderful friends. My heart leapt as his eyes sought mine while he spoke. Tears of joy, not pain, welled up inside me. He said this party was the most wonderful thing that had ever happened to him. My tears finally flowed when Mark wrapped me in his arms and kissed me, the first kiss in a long, long time. 'This is fantastic. I can't thank you enough, Lynne,' he whispered in my ear. His warm, muscular body felt so comfortable and right as I hugged him. I wanted to hold on forever.

A friend provided a big Roman candle, which we lit at dusk. The spectacular gold jets, shooting up into the night sky to our oohs and ahhs, made the perfect ending to a jubilant day.

From that night on, Mark and I were on the road back. Sure, we needed help, mostly from a counsellor who helped as Mark and I both strove for understanding on our often-difficult path to recovery. But the worst was over. We had won.

One evening a year after Mark's jubilee party, I heard Mark say to our minister, 'You know, there was a time when I was deeply depressed and God showed me love in an overwhelming way. That was a watershed moment for me.' As we drove home, I asked Mark what he had meant.

He looked at me, his eyebrows lifted in astonishment, and said, 'Why, the birthday party, of course. It showed me what I'd been too blind to see – that you still loved me, and what we had was worth saving. Lynne, that birthday party saved our marriage, and maybe it saved my life.'

GROWING PAINS

by Phyllis Hobe

In one moment of hate, she began to learn about love.

I loved everything about my Aunt Vera and wouldn't have changed her for the world. But I was very young and it never occurred to me that I might be the one who would undergo the change. When I was six years old, Aunt Vera was just turning twenty. But that didn't matter. We were best friends.

She was my father's younger sister and not yet married. She lived with my paternal grandparents and worked in an office as a secretary. She was very pretty: tall and graceful, with short curly black hair and blue eyes that laughed a lot.

Now, looking back, I can understand why we were best friends in spite of the difference in our ages. I was a child and Aunt Vera didn't want to grow up. The rest of our family thought it was time Aunt Vera started acting her age, but I liked her exactly the way she was. She was much more fun than any of the other grown-ups I knew. Besides, she actually preferred my company – on Saturdays, anyway – and I was proud of that. Not that she didn't have friends her own age. Aunt Vera was very popular and she could have done a lot of other things on Saturdays. But she didn't. She spent them with me.

She'd call for me right after lunch to take me shopping with her – not up to my local shops a few streets away, but in London, where the department stores were. It took us an hour to get to the city by bus and train. Yet the time went fast because we always had so much to talk about. Aunt Vera would tell me what she did in her office all week and I would tell her what I did in school.

Once we got to London we didn't buy much because Aunt Vera didn't have much money. But that wasn't the reason we went shopping, anyway. We went to look, so we didn't care if we couldn't have what we saw. If we liked something, we could imagine what fun it would be to have it. If we didn't like it, we could giggle. We did a lot of giggling, especially when we looked at dolls, because where dolls were concerned, we were experts.

'She's too snooty', was Aunt Vera's opinion of a princess-like creature in red velvet, warming her hands in a fuzzy white muff. I agreed. Neither of us was impressed by dolls whose eyes closed, the rage at the time. Or dolls with elaborately curled hair that, as Aunt Vera pointed out, would get pressed flat when you put them to bed at night. We both preferred soft, cuddly dolls, the kind you could really hug, and if you dropped them, their noses didn't chip. We would have been pushovers for Cabbage Patch Kids.

Before going home we always went to Woolworth's, which was the best part of our Saturdays. We'd have a drink, and then we'd go to the toy department so Aunt Vera could buy something for me. Aunt Vera had as much fun as I did picking out my toy. From her greater height she could survey a counter quickly and hold up, one by one, all the things she knew I liked: shiny bright-coloured metal jacks and a tiny rubber ball; a blue-and-white herringbone-patterned skipping rope with red handles; a bubble pipe with its own special cake of soap to squish in a bowl of water; full-skirted doll clothes wrapped in Cellophane; and – Aunt Vera's personal favourite – a book of paper dolls, a family of four, parents and two children, complete with a serviceable wardrobe, all of which I knew she would spend hours helping me cut out.

One Saturday, as I was finishing my drink and spinning around on the high cushioned stool at the counter, something caught my eye and appealed to me more than the toys we were about to visit. I had never noticed it before, but there was a gardening department in Woolworth's. I was particularly attracted to a display of seed packets, each one decorated with a coloured picture of the flowers that would – planted in the earth and warmed by the sun – magically sprout from the seeds.

Aunt Vera had paid for our drinks and was glancing in the direction of the toys. 'Hurry up, slow coach!' she said when she saw me hesitate. Then she came back to where I stood looking towards the gardening display. 'C'mon, honey,' she urged, reaching for my hand.

'Can I have some seeds instead?' I blurted out.

'Some what?'

'Some seeds. Over there. So I can grow flowers.'

Aunt Vera looked at where I was pointing, and I felt, for the first time in our relationship, a slight, impatient tug at my hand. 'But you can't,' she said. 'You live in a flat. You don't have a garden.'

'I'll find some soil,' I said. 'I can grow them on the windowsill.'

'They won't grow there.' Aunt Vera's pretty blue eyes weren't laughing. They were dark with disapproval and I had never seen them that way. She turned toward the toys which obviously still had their magic for her, but I pulled my hand free.

'They will grow! I'll water them every day!' I said.

Aunt Vera sighed and knelt down to look me straight in the eyes. 'Honey, you only think you want some seeds because it's springtime. But when they don't grow the way you want them to, you'll be disappointed.'

She didn't understand. For the first time in my life, Aunt Vera didn't feel the same way I felt.

She reached for my hand again. 'You'll have more fun with a skipping rope,' she said, standing up as if the matter had been settled.

I yanked my hand away and stepped back. 'No!' I said, louder than I meant to. Some customers nearby turned to look, but I was too upset to care what they thought. 'I don't want an old skipping rope! I don't want to go shopping with you anymore, either!'

I stopped abruptly then because I saw the pain in Aunt Vera's face. And I knew I had caused it. For a moment we stood facing each other, Aunt Vera with her eyes closed and her lips tight, my eyes wide with fear at what I had done.

Finally she spoke. 'We have to get our train,' she said.

I put my hand out stiffly and she took it. Her hand was cold.

Quite often the train was so crowded we had to sit apart. But that day we found seats together. We sat rigidly, being careful not to touch.

I felt physically ill. I really had – for a moment, at least – hated Aunt Vera, and I didn't want to believe that such a thing was possible. I wished with all my heart that we could go back to being the way we were. All I knew was that a packet of seeds had come between me and someone I loved dearly. I had come upon something I didn't know I had: a love to grow flowers. But I couldn't share that interest with Aunt Vera because she didn't feel the same way. And I no longer felt the same way about toys. Right there in the middle of Woolworth's I had started to grow up a little. I was changing. Aunt Vera was not.

But sitting next to her on the train that Saturday I realised, young as I was, that I still loved my Aunt Vera. For one terrible moment I had stopped loving her because she didn't want me to be different, and I had to be. But the moment didn't last. I didn't care if we weren't the same as we used to be. It didn't matter if sometimes we didn't like each other. Love doesn't always have to like.

It felt so good to love Aunt Vera again that I began to cry. Very quietly. I didn't want her to know.

She knew. She wasn't even looking at me, but she knew. She put her arm around me and pulled me close.

'I'm sorry,' I murmured.

'Don't be,' she said, kissing the top of my head. 'You're being yourself. That's wonderful.'

'Will you still love me?' I asked, holding my breath.

Her pretty blue eyes were smiling. 'Even more,' she said. 'And you know what?' I shook my head. 'I think I would be very happy if I did some growing up, too.' She hugged me closer. 'After all, I have to keep up with my best friend, don't I?'

We continued to go shopping on Saturdays until Aunt Vera got married a few years later. By the time I went to college, she was settled into family life. Our lives took different directions, and although we were never again as much alike as we once had been, we went on being each other's best friend. I think that's because we were able to recognise that people must change if they're to grow.

And so at that early age I learned that love stays the same. Like God, it is changeless – always accepting, forgiving, constant. It is we who do the changing. Keeping love in sight takes hard work. But it's the most worthwhile work God gives us to do.

A TEST OF FRIENDSHIP

by Faye Field

A simple task of washing dishes puts a woman through the wringer.

Nowadays, whenever I see an ad for a dishwashing detergent on TV, I find myself chuckling a little. I always think of my friend Kate and that day many years ago when washing dishes suddenly became something more than just a simple household task. I remember how I had hurried that afternoon. There were many chores at home needing to be done, but first there was Kate. She was recuperating from a bad bout of pneumonia, and I had promised to drop by with some food for her lunch on the days when my teaching schedule at the local college ended at noon.

On this particular day I stopped at a café on the city square to buy a lunch for Kate. I was pleased with my purchase. Tender peas, fresh corn, sirloin steak, hot rolls and Grape Nut pudding. Kate will have a nourishing meal, I thought as I drove along the shady street to her home.

I let myself in at the kitchen door, which was left unlocked in those days. I set the food down on the counter and called to Kate, taking time to push back my hair and flatten some stray locks. I always felt a little dowdy around Kate. She was so neat – never a hair out of place, never a wrinkle in her dress. That day I felt even more unkempt. I had dressed in a rush to get off to school. I remember just how attractive Kate looked coming from her bedroom to join me in the kitchen. Her dark hair was brushed to a glossy sheen. Her make-up was beautifully and delicately applied. Her illness in no way diminished her looking as if she had just come from the beauty salon or had stepped freshly from the pages of *Vogue* magazine. I don't think that I actually envied her; it was only that I felt uncomfortable by comparison. I was a little tired from rushing around.

'I've had a good rest. I stayed in bed all morning after my husband served me my breakfast and left for work,' Kate said as I made her a glass of iced tea to add to her lunch.

Kate was a wonderful conversationalist; I always enjoyed visiting her.

After she finished her lunch, we sat for a while and talked. Then I glanced at the unwashed dishes piled in the sink. 'Before I go home,' I said, 'I will wash those dishes along with the ones you have used here.'

'I'm sorry that those dinner dishes are still there,' Kate said. 'This morning Ray overslept and didn't have time to wash the breakfast dishes either. But I will help you. I'll sit here and dry the dishes as you wash. Someday soon we hope to have a dishwasher.' That's when the trouble started.

I removed the dishes from the sink, and the ones from the table, stacked them and was looking for the detergent to start the washing-up water when Kate interrupted me. 'I always scrape out all the crumbs first,' she said and smiled as she handed me a scraper.

I scraped off almost invisible particles with such vigour that the plates fairly shone.

Again I reached for the soap. Kate stopped me a second time. 'Wait just a minute, dear. Let's rinse these before we put them in the suds.' She smiled again.

So, I held the dishes under the tap, letting enough water flow freely over these to have furnished baths for a whole household.

At last I had the dish water ready.

I was beginning to immerse the already sparkling dishes. But then Kate put one flawlessly manicured hand in the waiting water.

'This water is not quite hot enough. I like the dishes to be well-scalded.' That smile again!

I let the hot water run until my hands turned lobster-red. Any hotter and I would have suffered third-degree burns.

After the dishes had been soaked and rinsed thoroughly, I thought that Kate would be ready to dry.

But we were not at the end yet.

'Let's run these through a second rinse just to be sure there's no soap build-up.' She smiled her endless smile. I doused the glistening dishes through another rinse. After this task, Kate began the drying. She examined each dish slowly and deliberately. She even handed back a fork that had a slight smudge for me to rewash. I could not imagine where that smear came from.

When the last dish was polished, I thought gratefully, *Now I can go home.*

I was wrong. There was one more job. Kate very carefully laid the silverware out on a fresh, dry tea towel. 'Let's let the silver air-dry a little while before putting it away.' Another smile, which by this time I was beginning to loathe.

I did not wait very long before I suggested, 'I really must leave. I need to do several things before my husband comes home from football practice. Is it all right if I put the silverware away now?'

Kate nodded and I placed the silver in the exact place she pointed out in the cabinet drawer.

I assisted her in getting back to bed. She thanked me, but her words did little to lessen my frustration at her fastidiousness.

As I drove home I kept frowning to myself about her being so picky, so inconsiderate of my time and her being so hard to please. I had barely reached home, kicked off my high-heeled shoes and stretched out for a few minutes to indulge in some self-pity, when a knock sounded at the back door.

What a nice surprise! There stood my eldest sister. She had driven from our home town about 130 miles away. Sister apologised. 'I tried to telephone you, but you weren't at home. So I came anyway. I hope it's okay.'

It was more than okay. By now I needed my sister. I needed someone I could let off steam with.

'I have had a trying time,' I started to say. 'I am very annoyed with Kate. You remember my friend, Kate Harris? She infuriated me. Today I sacrificed my time to help her. And all she did was make me feel dirty and sloppy. I can't believe anyone could be so demanding and contrary. She certainly had a strange way of showing her gratitude. I never did see anybody before make a three-act play out of a simple dishwashing.'

As I told Sister about the long, drawn-out dishwashing procedure, something odd began to happen. Every time I added a new detail about my frustration, Sister let out a little chuckle. I was dismayed. 'Kate has this cleanliness quirk,' I said in a protesting voice.

Chuckle.

'She had me do two rinses after that scalding dishwater,' I said.

Chuckle, chuckle.

'She not only towel-dried that silver, it had to be air-dried,' I went on.

And then, out of my own mouth, a most unexpected sound. Something suspiciously like a chuckle.

After that, with each comment I made – 'And I thought she'd never stop smiling!' – our laughter bubbled; until, when I'd finished, we were leaning back limply in our chairs – hugging our ribs.

'Honestly, if you hadn't come I would say she ruined this day for me,' I admitted.

Sister's smile widened. 'You want to know what I just thought of? It's a proverb I like a lot. "Being cheerful keeps you healthy." Because there are trying situations we face when we simply need to laugh.' She shook her head. 'It has to be funny, the way Kate washes dishes.'

My own head was beginning to nod. 'I guess that's the only way we can love the unlovable in people, to laugh at or with their idiosyncrasies.' I was starting to feel warm and friendly towards Kate once again. The resentment was gone. Or, at least, going. 'I hope folks will laugh at my eccentricities,' I said.

Our laughter flooded the kitchen and the room actually seemed to sparkle – just like Kate's thoroughly washed dishes!

THE LETTER

by Meryl McCotter

She loves his terrible golf.

Dear Bill,

You are in bed right now, but I can't go to sleep because I am thinking about our casual chat today about your golf score. I know that in spite of your joking about it, you don't enjoy losing as many times as you do. I want you to know, though, that I am proud of this score.

You were athletic in school so I have no doubts that you could become a good golfer. You could go out early each Saturday morning as so many of your golfing mates do and eventually become as good as or better than any of them.

But I remember the Saturday you helped to set up tables at the local hall. I remember the Saturday you planned a trip – it was one you'd taken, but you felt that the kids and I would enjoy it. Other Saturdays you felt that you should travel the 200 miles to your widowed mother's home to take care of the repairs and chores she might not be able to do for herself.

Oh, yes, Sunday is the other day of the week that you might have been using to improve that golf score, but, no, come 9.45 a.m. you have to be prepared to teach a Sunday-school class. After that you might be free to dash out to the greens, but then who would sit in the congregation with your own littlies while your wife sings in the choir?

I could go on, but I just wanted you to know that when your wife thinks of your golf score, she is tremendously proud. Someday it might be improved, but in the meantime it stands as a symbol of the love and respect your family feels for you.

Your wife,
Meryl

FORGET ME NOT

by Grayce Bonham Confer

Her beautiful Valentine.

Harold, my husband, has Alzheimer's disease. At first it was little things I noticed: not buttoning his shirt properly or forgetting to zip his trousers. Then there were bigger lapses of memory. He would start a sentence and then look at me, not knowing what he was going to say. He'd look at television and then walk around behind it, trying to figure out how the person there got into the room.

All of these things were painful to see, but for me the worst was watching Harold slip further and further away. How I yearned for the wonderful, caring Harold of old. How I longed to feel my husband's love again.

On February fourteenth I went to pick up Harold at the local adult day-care centre where it had been arranged for him to go each day. A nurse handed me a folded square of paper. The group, she told me, had spent the afternoon in crafts making Valentines. 'Your husband made this,' the nurse said. 'I think it's for you.'

The Valentine was bordered with grey lace on the edges and a large red heart set in the centre, surrounded by frilly white paper doilies. A bow of red yarn adorned one corner.

'It's beautiful, darling,' I said to Harold. Then I opened the fold of the Valentine. There was a jumble of red crayoned jiggly marks inside. The vaguest sort of chicken scratching.

At first the marks seemed meaningless to me, but I looked closer. They were words: Ich liebe dich ... German words, and I knew what they meant.

I had known those words for fifty years, ever since our courting days at the university. Harold had always ended his little notes the same way: Ich liebe dich besten, für Ewigkeit und Ewigkeit (I love you best, forever and forever).

It was the most beautiful Valentine I had ever received. He loved me then. And this I knew: he loved me still.

THE LOVE WE'VE FOUND

by Ann Sayer

True love is never paralysed.

I really didn't feel comfortable as I walked through the respirator ward. As a volunteer hospital visitor, I certainly shouldn't have had such an attitude, but the utter hopelessness of the patients made me want to cry. And then I saw the curtained cubicle where the leather bellows of an iron lung ballooned in and out.

The patient, a quadriplegic, had intrigued me when I had visited this ward previously. There was an independent look in his eyes and something almost defiant in his voice.

'Hi, my name's Ann. Remember me?' I said, urging a cheerful note into my voice.

Bill was reading a book fastened to a rack above his head. 'Hello,' he mumbled around a rubber-tipped mouth stick with which he turned the pages. Two sky-blue eyes regarded me.

I removed my coat. 'Dark in here, isn't it?' I reached for the window shade. 'There, that's better, isn't it?'

'Yeah.' He sounded convinced he was about to be pestered.

'Would you like your mirror?'

'Okay.'

I exchanged the reading rack for his mirror. They both fit into the same bracket on the front of the iron lung.

Finally I was seated, peering up into the respirator mirror through which Bill viewed the world. He had a thin, good-looking face, Roman nose and red hair. 'How did you get sick?' I asked.

'I got polio. I'm in an iron lung. That's all there is to it.'

I swallowed and tried again. 'When did you contract polio?'

'Fifteen years ago. I was twenty when it hit me.' Doctor Salk's vaccine had come too late for him.

I felt a chill as I realised that for fifteen years a motor impassively had kept Bill's flesh, blood and lungs functioning.

For the next hour, I carried on a monologue punctuated by single syllable answers. It was hard work, but something made me keep trying. Finally, I said, 'I guess I'll be going.'

'Okay,' he said. 'Before you go, would you turn on my TV?'

I flipped it on.

'Take care,' I said, struggling into my coat.

'Sure. Be good.' I felt dismissed. He was intent on the television screen.

My eyes blurred as I rushed into the cold night. But later at home, as I sipped hot coffee, I realised Bill couldn't enjoy such a haven. He could not go to a quiet place and meditate. Bill lived in a fish bowl. He had to be fed, bathed, and assisted to perform the most intimate functions.

I admired him. He was embarrassingly honest, making clear what he liked and didn't like, without apology. His refusal to give in to self-pity showed me he had not succumbed to despair.

I knew how easy that could be. I was thirty-two, unmarried, and like Bill, was putting up a brave pretence of not needing anyone. Despite his crusty attitude, I decided to go back to the hospital to see him again.

I returned the following weekend bringing sandwiches and coffee. Bill dropped his guard a little and our conversation flowed easier. I learned that he was an avid reader and had always wanted to be a writer. Soon our visits became a weekly occurrence. When Bill's meals arrived, it seemed natural that I feed him.

I began to look forward to the visits.

Our talk often turned to Bill's writing ambitions. 'God left me with a healthy mind,' he said, 'and a love of books. But I don't know a thing about the mechanics of writing.'

'Why not take a short-story correspondence course?' I suggested.

His head turned and his eyes brightened. 'You think I could?'

'Sure,' I laughed. 'You can dictate to me and I'll type up the lessons and mail them.'

When the course started, I began visiting him every day. They were busy days, full of Bill's dictation and my typing the lessons and mailing them. Through it all I watched his native ability grow. At first his writing scrupulously followed the course instructions, then it began to flow as his confidence strengthened.

One day another volunteer invited Bill and me to a party at her home. To my surprise, Bill accepted the invitation.

To leave the hospital, Bill had to wear a portable chest respirator. This was a plastic shell that hugged his body from abdomen to chest. From it a hose snaked to a bulky compressor motor on wheels.

When he was lifted to the stretcher for the trip, I saw his legs. They were encrusted with bedsores, and he groaned when he was moved. Then Bill, strapped to the stretcher, and I, with my legs shaking at the possibility of his respirator failing, were off to the party.

We enjoyed ourselves, or rather, Bill enjoyed himself. The thought of an emergency didn't bother him at all. Once in a while, a grimace of pain crossed his face, but he did not complain.

I was relieved when we returned to the hospital.

'How did you like it, Ann?' His smile was eager.

'Fine,' I lied.

'Would you ease my chest strap, please?' he asked. I began to loosen the belt. His face crumpled with relief. 'Too tight all day,' he said.

'Why didn't you tell me?'

'It was nothing. Everything went great, right?' He smiled brightly. 'It isn't hard to get me out of the hospital, see?'

I didn't answer as I continued adjusting the belt. All I could remember was his sore legs, his pain, his helplessness.

'Ann, will you marry me?'

My hands froze. So that was it! He had made the trip to show he could safely leave the hospital.

In a daze I completed his belt adjustment, and forced myself to speak. 'I ... uh ... I really don't know how to answer, Bill,' I stammered. 'Give me a little time to think.'

I could see the disappointment in his eyes. But then he bravely covered it up. 'Don't take it too seriously, Ann ... guess I had too much grape juice at the party.'

In my apartment that night I could only think about Bill's proposal. One thing I knew: I loved him. Deeply, surely. For months now I had known it. And his proposal really wasn't that much of a surprise.

In our visits I could feel Bill's fondness for me growing. I could see him reaching out for life and love after all his bitter years behind the walls of the hospital. He needed me and I loved him.

But could we manage? Did I have the courage to try?

Bill had many physical ailments, any one of which could lead to an emergency situation. From years in the iron lung, his joints had stiffened. His muscles sprained easily and his bones were frail and brittle so that even giving him a bath took hours of gentle, slow handling.

A simple cold could develop into pneumonia. His breathing equipment broke down periodically and required immediate attention by a mechanic. Power failures were frequent in the area where we would have to live, as close to the hospital as possible.

I would have to quit work and we would live on his Social Security disability cheques and supplementary welfare. We would move into public housing.

I rose and walked to the window, looking into the rainy night. No, I couldn't do it. It was more than human strength could bear. The life Bill had to accept for fifteen years was too hard.

And then I looked back on my last fifteen years; carefree, pointless, empty. And suddenly I knew I faced a decision. Life or death.

Marrying Bill would be accepting the cross that is at the heart of all vital living. To be alive is to suffer sometimes. Suffering isn't all there is to life, but unless we accept misery as an integral part of it, all the other experiences are diminished. And suffering is unbearable only when we feel alone in it.

So I chose life, I chose Bill.

Nine years ago we were married.

Bill is now a happy guy constantly involved in some new project. He's still paralysed from the shoulders down, but is no longer dependent on the iron lung. He breathes through an air tube. 'I can do just about anything,' he says, grinning up at me.

And Bill is pursuing his writing career, typing three or four hours every day, striking the keys of an electric typewriter with a mouth stick. He has completed a book about his years in the hospital. A literary agent read the manuscript and said it has merit. After repeated attempts to sell it, we finally found a publisher for it.

Recently I showed a friend some snapshots I had taken of Bill. After scanning them, she said, 'You can see the happiness shining out of his face.'

'Yes,' I said, 'I know I have it, too.'

And I do. Oh, yes; I do.

THE CHILD NOBODY WANTED

by Elizabeth Sherrill

A small boy's childhood starts again.

Peter was not a 'lovable' child. Since his parents had died, he had
been shuttled from one family to another, not wanted, not belong-
ing. Now, at age five, he was protecting himself from a world that
didn't want him, by hating that world. Peter wouldn't talk, he
wouldn't smile, he hated everybody.

At the Hillcrest Adoption Centre, they had just about given up
finding a home for Peter. My friend Isobel Clarke is a caseworker
there. She talked to me often about Peter.

'It would take a miracle to make that boy risk loving someone
again,' she said.

And then one day Mrs Greene came to the Centre. Mrs Greene
told Isobel that she and her husband had waited fifteen years for
a child of their own; now they knew there wouldn't be one. Isobel
hardly heard her; she was looking into Mrs Greene's face, thinking
she had never seen a face so full of love. And as she looked at her,
Isobel was thinking, 'Peter'.

She told Mrs Green about him and saw her eyes shine at the
idea of having a little boy of her own. 'But I'm frightened,' Isobel
admitted to me, 'Peter is such a badly hurt little boy. Mrs Greene
won't believe me when I tell her that he hates everybody. She
hasn't seen him yet.'

It was a long time before Mrs Greene could see Peter. First there had to be interviews, medical reports, family histories – the Adoption Service puts 'parents' and children together with infinite pains before they are ever allowed to meet.

But at last the great day came when Mrs Greene was to see Peter for the first time. Peter was taken to the public park 'to play on the swings'. Mrs Greene and Isobel were to sit down on one of the benches where Mrs Greene could watch him without his knowing that he was being 'considered'. As Isobel walked with Mrs Greene to the park, her heart was pounding so hard she was afraid Mrs Greene would hear it. She knew, as she'd never known anything before, that this woman and this little boy belonged together. 'But, dear God, let them know it too,' she prayed as they neared the gate. 'Don't let her see just his silent, angry little face! Don't let this first meeting be so bad it spoils the rest!'

For there would be other meetings of course: another 'chance' meeting next time with Mr Greene as well, then a visit to Peter's boarding home, then … But so much depended on this first time!

They were through the gate now, and Isobel saw Peter a little way off, near the swings. He wasn't swinging, he was standing next to the fence, his eyes on the ground.

Isobel turned with an encouraging smile to Mrs Greene, but she had forgotten Isobel was there. Her eyes were fixed on Peter.

Then Mrs Greene was walking straight to him. *No, no!* thought Isobel, hurrying after her. *This was all wrong! Peter must never guess that she was watching him!* Mrs Greene was almost running now. Peter looked up and saw her, and he too started running – not away, but straight to her.

Now they stopped, a foot apart, neither of them speaking, just looking at each other. Isobel caught up with them.

'Peter,' she said, 'do you know who this lady is?'

'Yes,' said Peter. His eyes never left Mrs Greene's face as he said, 'She's my mother.'

FRAGILE MOMENTS

by Galen Drake

Words are very powerful when used with love.

My favourite love story is also a true one. Soon after he was married, Thomas Moore, the famous nineteenth century Irish poet, was called away on a business trip. Upon his return he was met at the door not by his beautiful bride, but by the family doctor.

'Your wife is upstairs,' said the doctor. 'But she has asked that you do not come up.' And then Moore learned the terrible truth: his wife had contracted smallpox. The disease had left her once flawless skin pocked and scarred. She had taken one look at her reflection in the mirror and commanded that the shutters be drawn and that her husband never see her again.

Moore would not listen. He ran upstairs and threw open the door of his wife's room. It was black as night inside. Not a sound came from the darkness. Groping along the wall, Moore felt for the gas jets.

A startled cry came from a black corner of the room. 'No! Don't light the lamps!'

Moore hesitated, swayed by the pleading in the voice.

'Go!' she begged. 'Please go! This is the greatest gift I can give you, now.'

Moore did go. He went down to his study where he sat up most of the night writing. Not a poem this time, but a song. He had never written a song before, but now he found it more natural to his mood than simple poetry. He not only wrote the words, he wrote the music too. And the next morning as soon as the sun was up he returned to his wife's room.

He felt his way to a chair and sat down. 'Are you awake?' he asked.

'I am,' came a voice from the far side of the room. 'But you must not ask to see me. You must not press me, Thomas.'

'I will sing to you, then,' he answered. And so, for the first time, Thomas Moore sang to his wife the song that still lives today:

Believe me, if all those endearing young charms,
Which I gaze on so fondly today,
Were to change by tomorrow,
and flee in my arms,
Like fairy gifts fading away,
Thou wouldst still be adored,
as this moment thou art
Let thy loveliness fade as it will,

Moore heard a movement from the dark corner where his wife lay in her loneliness, waiting. He continued:

Let thy loveliness fade as it will,
And around the dear ruin each wish of my heart
Would entwine itself verdantly still....

The song ended. As his voice trailed off on the last note, Moore heard his bride rise. She crossed the room to the window, reached up and slowly drew open the shutters.

THE PRACTICAL THING TO DO

by Madge Harrah

Aged parents are shown their true value.

A cold night wind buffeted the bedroom windows, hurling sleet against the glass. My father looked up from his pillow and rasped in a hoarse voice, 'Madge, I finally have to admit it – your mother and I just can't live here in our own home any longer. You're going to have to take the bull by the horns and put us in the nursing home.'

My parents' doctor had said much the same thing to me earlier that day, but my heart still thudded with shock at my father's words. The one thing my aged parents had wanted during the past several months was to be allowed to live their remaining days together at home, surrounded by their own things. I glanced toward my mother, who lay next to my father, sharing his bed as she had throughout a lifetime of marriage. Once tall and plump, she was now thin and shrunken from osteoporosis.

A few days earlier I had arrived here at my parents' home to help with their nursing care.

My father had come down with pneumonia and incipient congestive heart failure, and my mother had developed influenza. Although they managed to pull through that crisis, their doctor had warned me that they probably would not live much longer.

'How do you feel about the nursing home, Mum?' I now asked.

I watched her fingers creep across the sheets to clasp my father's large work-worn hand.

'I'll do whatever you and your father decide,' she said.

This is it, I told myself, still not believing it could be true. The time has finally come.

I had been hoping along with them that such a decision would never have to be made. I glanced around the bedroom, which was filled with some of their favourite things: their comfortable large bed with their special individual pillows; the patterned quilt they both liked; my father's brown walnut desk; his old manual Remington typewriter, the large blue vase he had bought as a gift for my mother; and on the walls, some of Mother's best paintings, her gifts to my father. How could my parents be peaceful and happy in any room but this?

'I put our names on the waiting list for the nursing home three years ago,' Dad said, his voice taking on some of the authority and strength he had used in the classroom throughout forty years of teaching. 'It's time to put us away.'

I had visited that nursing home, which was run by some of my parents' former students. The home was clean, the staff well-trained, the food nourishing, the atmosphere cheerful. If I put my parents there, I knew they would get good care. I have always believed that people should not feel guilty about placing a loved one in a nursing home. Sometimes a nursing home is the best answer. But in this instance I resisted the idea. For one thing, I was my parents' only surviving child, and I lived several hundred miles away. If they went into that nursing home, they would have no relatives nearby to visit and check on them.

'But I want – ' I began.

Dad lifted a hand to stop me. 'Look, I know you keep saying we can come and live with you, but it isn't practical. We've got to be practical.'

Practical – one of his favourite words.

'Your home is a long way off,' he went on. 'We're too sick to travel that far. You've got your own family at home to take care of.

No, the practical thing is to put us in that nursing home and not look back.'

Dad was right; that was the practical thing to do. Then why did I feel so terrible about it? And why did he look so forlorn?

Barely audible above the clamour of the wind and sleet outside, I heard my mother murmur, 'I'm going to miss this bed.'

Unable to bear their pain any longer, and knowing they both liked a cup of something hot at bedtime, I said, 'I'll go make a pot of decaf coffee.'

Turning, I fled from the room. After plugging in the coffee pot, I wandered down the hallway and into the living room, where I nervously picked things up and set them down again. My head pounded, my hands trembled. Never had I felt so helpless or so alone. *All right, God, I need some help here,* I begged in silent despair. *Are you listening?*

The only answer was the howling of the storm shaking the house, shaking me. I touched a drawer handle that my practical father had screwed to the wall at hand level. At regular intervals throughout the house were other drawer handles screwed to the walls, put there by my father when he first started losing his balance due to inner-ear trouble. The handles helped him to walk from one room to another; he could pull himself from handhold to handhold without fear of falling down. Yes, he was practical, all right. Practical and logical, as a math teacher should be.

Okay, then, let's be practical, whispered a cold, hard voice in the back of my head. If they go into the nursing home, you're off the hook. No bedpans to empty, no lost sleep, no watching them fade away. They're too weak to travel, if you take them home you'll have to hire a van with a bed for them to lie down on, and you'll have to bring oxygen along. They might die on the trip...

But Dad didn't really want to go into that nursing home. Mother had told me so in private, but I would have known it anyway, just from the lost look in his eyes when he talked about it.

On the other hand, moving them to my home would be messy and difficult, and certainly impractical.

'God, you've got to help me!' I cried aloud. 'I can't stand this! What's the best thing to do?'

Still no answer.

I wandered on into the dining room where some of Mother's drawings lay scattered on the table, simple line drawings on cardboard. She had made them for the children's Sunday school classes at her church to illustrate various Bible verses. I glanced idly over them and then stopped, arrested by one drawing in particular. It showed a soaring mansion that reached into the clouds. The verse from John's Gospel lettered below read, 'There are many rooms in my Father's house, and I am going to prepare a place for you. I would not tell you this if it were not so. And after I go and prepare a place for you, I will come back and take you to myself, so that you will be where I am.'

It was as though light flowed into me, bringing with it a stilling of the storm, a sense of peace. There it was – the answer I'd been asking for.

I scribbled a note to myself and hurried back into my parents' bedroom.

'Now listen,' I said to them both. 'I will have to put you into that nursing home for the time being, until you get some of your strength back. But meanwhile, I'll hire a van to take all this' – and I swept my hand through the air to include everything in the room – 'to my home. I'll fix up a room in our house, with all your things in it, and when the room is ready and the weather warms up, I'll be back to get you.' Although they tried to smile, I saw the doubt on their faces. Would I come back for them? They weren't certain.

Nevertheless, a few weeks later my husband, Lee, and I came back, hired a van, and drove my mother and father to our home. The night we arrived, I carried a tray with a pot of coffee and two cups into their bedroom, where they lay side by side in their own bed, their special pillows under their heads and their patterned quilt over their frail bodies. Against one wall sat my father's desk and typewriter, along with the big blue vase, and hanging above the desk was my mother's painting of a pot of wildflowers.

'Totally impractical,' my father said gruffly when I appeared in the doorway. Six weeks later my father went to live in the room God had prepared, and four months after that my mother followed.

Recently, in going though some boxes that Lee and I brought back after clearing out my parents' home, I came across the note I had scribbled to myself that stormy night after getting the answer to my problem. The note read: 'Sometimes the wise, sensible, practical solution to a problem is not the best because it leaves out love. Sometimes the illogical, difficult, expensive, messy solution is the best because it's the only way love can be satisfied.'

I had chosen the loving solution, and somehow I think my father may have agreed – it was the practical solution after all.

A MAN OF FEW WORDS

by Bertrand Clompus

Why couldn't he say what his son so longed to hear?

After my mother died, I began visiting my father every morning before I went to work. He was frail and moved slowly, but he always had a glass of freshly squeezed orange juice on the kitchen table for me, along with an unsigned note reading, 'Drink your juice'.

Such a gesture, I knew, was as far as Dad had ever been able to go in expressing his love. In fact, I remember, as a kid I had questioned Mum: 'Why doesn't Dad love me?'

Mum frowned. 'Who said he doesn't love you?'

'Well, he never tells me,' I complained.

'He never tells me either,' she said, sympathising with a smile. 'But look how hard he works to take care of us, to buy us food and clothes, and to pay for this house. That's how your father tells us he loves us.' Then Mum held me by the shoulders and asked, 'Do you understand?'

I nodded slowly. I understood in my head, but not in my heart. I still wanted my father to put his arms around me and tell me he loved me.

Dad owned and operated a small scrap-metal business, and after school I often hung around while he worked. I always hoped he'd ask me to help and then praise me for what I did. He never asked. His tasks were too dangerous for a young boy to attempt, and Mum was already worried enough that he'd hurt himself.

59

Dad hand-fed scrap steel into a device that chopped it as cleanly as a butcher chops a rack of ribs. The machine looked like a giant pair of scissors, with blades thicker than my father's body. If he didn't feed those terrifying blades just right, he risked serious injury.

'Why don't you hire someone to do that for you?' Mum asked Dad one night as she bent over him and rubbed his aching shoulders with a strong-smelling liniment.

'Why don't you hire a cook?' Dad asked, giving her one of his rare smiles.

Mum straightened and put her hands on her hips. 'What's the matter, don't you like my cooking?'

'Sure I like your cooking! But if I could afford a helper, then you could afford a cook!' Dad laughed, and for the first time I realised that my father had a sense of humour.

The chopping machine wasn't the only hazard in his business. He had an acetylene torch for cutting thick steel plates and beams. To my ears the torch hissed louder than a steam locomotive, and when he used it to cut through steel, it blew off thousands of tiny pieces of molten metal that swarmed around him like angry fireflies.

Dad wore heavy leather gloves, dark goggles and a wide-brimmed hat, but one day the torch set his socks on fire. He came home with painful blisters on his ankles that Mum helped him cover with thick yellow ointment.

'Why can't you be more careful?' Mum demanded, her voice full of concern.

'What do you want me to do, Molly, work standing all day in a tub of water?' Dad parried.

They began laughing and I couldn't understand how my father could joke about something like that. Of course, I realised later it was the best thing he could do to help Mum stop worrying, to get them both through those hard years.

At the beginning of each day, Dad faithfully opened his prayer book and read a portion of it. He always stood in a corner of our living room, his yarmulke a little tilted and his shoulders slightly swaying in rhythm to the same ancient prayers his father and grandfathers had said before him.

One morning he ended his prayers by putting down his prayer book, raising his arms to God and softly asking, 'Do you think you could make things a little easier for me?' At that moment my usually stoic and uncomplaining father looked so vulnerable that I wanted to throw my arms around him and protect him.

Many years later, during my daily visit, I did just that. After drinking the juice my father had squeezed for me, I walked over, hugged him and said, 'I love you, Dad.' From then on I did this every morning.

My father never told me how he felt about my hugs, and there was never any expression on his face when I gave them. Then one morning, pressed for time, I drank my juice and made for the door.

Dad stepped in front of me and asked. 'Well?'

'Well what?' I asked, knowing exactly what.

'Well?' he repeated, crossing his arms and looking everywhere but at me.

I hugged him extra hard. Now was the right time to say what I'd always wanted to.

'I'm fifty years old, Dad, and you've never told me you love me.'

My father stepped away from me. He picked up the empty juice glass, washed it and put it away.

'You've told other people you love me,' I said, 'but I've never heard it from you.'

Dad looked uncomfortable. Very uncomfortable.

I moved closer to him. 'Dad, I want you to tell me you love me.'

Dad took a step back, his lips pressed together. He seemed about to speak, then shook his head.

'Tell me!' I shouted.

'All right! I love you!' Dad finally blurted, his hands fluttering like wounded birds. And in that instant something occurred that I had never seen happen in my life: His eyes glistened, then overflowed.

I stood before him, stunned and silent. Finally, after all these years, my heart joined my head in understanding. My father loved me so much that just saying so made him weep, which was something he never, ever wanted to do, least of all in front of family. Mum had been right. Every day of my life Dad had told me how much he loved me by what he did and what he gave. 'I know, Dad,' I said. 'I know.'

And now at last I did.

DON'T LET THEM STOP LOVING ME

by Jan Turner

Could she be a mother anymore?

I've always loved children; that's one reason I became a teacher.

Yet I knew I had much more to give. Even though I had enjoyed being single, I wanted to share the love in my heart with some child who did not have a family. So in the early 1980s I began the rigorous application procedures to adopt.

After months of interviews and psychological evaluations, I was allowed to adopt six-year-old Tyler from a Brazilian government orphanage. Two years later Cody joined us. I taught music full-time at a college school and was music director at our church. On weekends and in the summer I took the boys camping, fishing, hiking. We were happy and busy, and I was thinking about adopting a third child. I loved being a mum.

One Sunday in November 1989 I was playing trumpet in church as the boys beamed at me from a front pew. Suddenly I felt weak, dizzy and nauseated. *I'm going to have to sit down before I fall,* I thought. I had to leave before I collapsed. I motioned the boys to follow me out. Driving home I prayed silently, Lord, just let me get the boys home safely.

Dad often stopped over on Sundays after church to spend time with the boys and me. That particular Sunday he found me in bed aching and shivering – in terrible pain. I continued to get worse into the night. By the time he got me to the hospital I was comatose. My liver and kidneys went into distress; my blood pressure dropped so severely that my body was in danger of shutting down.

The doctors diagnosed pneumococcal pneumonia, a swift and deadly bacterial infection, the same illness that took the life of Muppets creator Jim Henson. My body had gone into a last-ditch survival mode, cutting off blood and oxygen to my hands and feet in order to preserve vital organs. On top of all this, Dad fell and was hospitalised, so the boys were put in the care of a church friend. What would become of them if something happened to me?

After two weeks, my doctor came in and sat on my bed. 'Jan, there's no good way to tell you this.' She took a deep breath. 'Your arms and legs will have to be amputated. The arms at mid-forearm and legs at mid-shin.'

I couldn't speak. I bit my lower lip. Oh, God, no! How can I live without feet and hands? Never walk again? Never play the trumpet, guitar, piano or any of the instruments I teach? How can I take care of my sons?

Even though the doctor told me I could walk with prosthetics, I envisioned myself helpless, completely dependent on others. Oh, Lord, maybe the boys would be better off without me.

A day later I was a quadruple amputee. At the end of the week, when I was taken out of intensive care, the doctor said my boys could visit me for the first time since I had entered the hospital.

I was apprehensive. I wanted desperately to look as normal as possible so that Tyler and Cody wouldn't be shocked. On the day of their visit I asked a nurse to fix my hair and prop me up in a chair beside my bed. Then I heard my sister, Maureen, bringing the boys down the hall.

Suddenly they appeared at the doorway, frightened looks in their eyes. I wanted to reach my arms out to them, yet I was weak and afraid to make any gesture that would call attention to my stumps. When I smiled and called their names, they approached me cautiously. A few feet from my chair Cody stopped and cried out, 'You're not my mum! My mum has arms and legs!'

The breath went out of me and my body went limp. I thought I would slide out of the chair onto the floor. Tears welled in my eyes. *Oh, God, give me courage. Help my sons know I'm still their mum. Don't let them stop loving me!*

The days dragged by. I remained totally dependent on others. How could I make a life for myself with Tyler and Cody? Lord, I need your help.

One day Maureen brought her minister to see me. Almost directly he put his hands on my shoulders and said, 'Jan, believe that God gives good gifts, a verse in the Bible says: "Fix our attention, not on things that are seen, but on things that are unseen"' (2 Corinthians 4:18).

A rehabilitation specialist explained all about artificial limbs. She told me I could learn to walk, drive a car, even go back to teaching. *How can that be possible?* I wondered.

Later when a nurse put my Bible on my tray in front of me. I began reading where it fell open: 'Let God transform you inwardly by a complete change of your mind' (Romans 12:2). A warm feeling tingled down my spine. It was as if the words had been placed before me. I was certainly different – whole parts of me were missing! But I felt encouraged. I just had to learn to begin again.

So I began. Not long afterwards my first set of artificial legs was ready. I wasn't prepared for the pain I felt when my body weight pushed my stumps against the prosthetics. With a walker strapped onto my forearms near the elbow, and the support of two physical therapists, I could wobble on my new legs for only two or three minutes before I collapsed in exhaustion and pain.

Take it slowly, I said to myself. I had always been an impulsive, do-it-now type. *You've got to be new in patience too.*

The next day I tried on my arms – a strange combination of cables, rubber bands and hooks activated by a harness across my shoulders. By flexing my shoulder muscles I was able to open and close the hooks. Every morning and afternoon for the next two months I was in the occupational therapy room practising picking up objects, dressing and feeding myself.

Since my therapists hadn't worked with a quadruple amputee before, we mastered some procedures together. I began to feel really good because I was helping them learn things they'd be able to use with future patients. Other tricks the therapists already knew: putting shampoo on a flannel to wash my hair, applying styling gel right on a hairbrush, and leaning on a wall to keep my balance while pulling a jumper off.

As I got used to the prosthetics, I came to appreciate some hidden benefits. Ever since I was a teenager I'd disliked two things – not being tall and having freezing hands and feet during the winter. So as new prosthetics were custom fitted for me, I had the legs made longer. Now I'm five feet eight! And I'm the only person I know who can be toasty warm in mid-January wearing thin socks and no gloves and who can take a piping hot casserole from the oven without a pot holder.

My main therapist told me I could go home when I was able to perform most normal household tasks. 'That includes carrying an egg across a room without breaking it,' one said, 'and flipping pancakes.'

'But I never could flip a pancake,' I protested.

'Well, then,' she replied with a wink, 'it's high time you learned.'

By mid-March, nearly four months after I was hospitalised, my therapists were satisfied. That first day out I joined the boys in walking our dogs. The next day I got up early. By the time the boys sat down at the breakfast table I was already cooking pancakes. I could tell they were impressed.

'Hey, kids,' I said, 'watch this!'

And I flipped a pancake right onto Cody's plate.

'Mum, that's really neat,' he said.

And so was being a mum again.

Headway

Do not let fear confine your life
Inside a shell of doubt;
A turtle never moves until
His head is sticking out.

Charles Ghigna

2

WHEN FEAR
IS BROKEN

*Fear is my dreaded enemy. It haunts me
whenever it gets the chance. Only faith and trust
can prevent it from lurking and send it scuttling
from the secret crevices of my mind.*

Wendy Craig

BETWEEN HEAVEN
AND EARTH

by Mark Monsino

It was certain death from 3000 feet.

I knew that in a moment I would be dead. I looked down and saw the ground rushing up at me. There was no way I could save myself. I heard myself say, 'Oh, God, help me.'

It was the first time I had asked God for anything. All my life I had taken care of myself. I believed in God and I went to church, but this was merely a habit I inherited from my parents, a habit I practised without giving it any thought.

When the machine shop where I worked went out of business and I was suddenly out of a job, it never occurred to me to turn to God. After all, this was my life, and it was up to me to find myself another job.

But months passed and I was still unemployed. I was twenty-two, still living at home, and was becoming a burden to my family. I had always supported myself ever since I was old enough to peddle newspapers, and now I was borrowing money and piling up debts. Finally I took the only job that came along, as a deckhand on a cabin cruiser going to Florida.

In Florida, I had a little money in my pocket, but I was again out of a job, again spending my days looking for one. One day a friend of mine happened to say, 'There's a guy I know who has a sky-diving school.'

The idea of skydiving had fascinated me for a long time. I knew it was becoming an increasingly popular sport, and the thought struck me that if I became good enough at it maybe I could get a job teaching it. I went over to the school and signed up.

The little private airport was near a farm in the quiet and beautiful open countryside. There were seven of us in the skydiving class. We had four hours of instruction on the ground – the fundamentals of controlling a parachute to make it carry you where you wanted to go; how to make the chute 'hold', 'run' or 'crab'; timing your dive; positioning your body – all the do's and don'ts of diving from an aeroplane. Then we had to pass a written examination.

We were ready for our first jump – four students, the instructor and pilot in the sleek Cessna 189. I was dressed in the regulation jumping gear – a red denim overall, a motorcycle helmet and shock-absorbing jumping boots. In my parachute pack on my back was a red, white and blue main chute and the smaller reserve chute for emergencies.

'Check all your gear,' the instructor ordered. 'Always make sure all the straps are secure, neither too tight nor too loose.'

We were flying at 3200 feet over grassy cattle farms with irrigation ditches running through them, and on the ground ahead, near the end of the airport, I could see the circular hole in the ground filled with white sand that looked like a sand trap on a golf course. That was the soft landing zone where I was to try to land.

'Okay, Mark. Go!' the instructor shouted.

I leapt out the cabin door, arched my back, spread out my arms and legs, and began counting very slowly. 'One, two, three, four, five.'

The first instant when I stepped out into space was a bit scary, like falling in a dream; but then it was the most beautiful feeling I have ever experienced, falling through the air, a wonderful floating feeling, looking down at the earth as an eagle does, completely detached and free.

Then I pulled the ripcord and, with a snap and a jerk, my red, white and blue chute unfurled and billowed out behind me and opened into a glorious canopy that held me suspended in space. I drifted down and landed with a thud – not the best of landings and not on the white sand, but safe and sound.

From that moment on I was hooked, a skydiving addict. I couldn't get enough of it, the thrill, the excitement, the beautiful feeling of flying through the air as free and on one's own as a man can be. It was a wonderful exhilaration. In a way, as I spread my arms and soared through the air, I felt I was living out my attitude about myself: independent, self-reliant, self-sufficient, in control.

Eleven times I jumped, and each time it was a wonderful thrill, a glorious feeling I find hard to describe.

My twelfth skydive was on 19 June 1977. It was a beautiful sunny Sunday afternoon, a few white clouds and a very light breeze, a perfect day for skydiving. Once again there were six of us aboard the Cessna – four divers, the instructor and pilot. I was still a student, but beginning to feel like a veteran eager to do the more advanced stunts of skydiving.

We took off and the pilot lined up at 3600 feet for the first jumper. He dived out, fell with his arms and legs outspread for ten seconds, then pulled the ripcord. His chute opened perfectly and he floated down to a good landing.

Each man jumps on a separate pass, and I was the second to jump that day. We circled around and came back on the path toward the white sand target, flying at 3600 feet. When we were about a quarter mile from the landing target the instructor yelled: 'Go!' And out I went.

Once again I had the wonderful feeling of sailing through the air as I counted out the seconds – ten this time, as I had jumped from a higher altitude. A huge forest was spread out below me, but I was looking ahead to the patch of white where I intended to land.

Absolutely essential in skydiving is maintaining the proper position of your body. You must keep your back arched with your arms and legs spread wide and backwards. This keeps you facing the direction of your fall and maintains your stability. I knew quite a few skydivers had been killed, but I didn't consider skydiving dangerous, not any more dangerous than crossing a busy street.

'Seven, eight, nine ...' Suddenly I realised that I had lost my arched position. Instead of floating in an almost horizontal spread-eagle position, I was falling head-down at 120 miles an hour. 'Ten!' I pulled the ripcord.

My main parachute streamed out of my back pack, but instead of opening, the shroud lines became tangled around my legs. I had now fallen 1000 feet and was plummeting towards the earth at over 100 feet a second. I immediately pulled the ripcord on my reserve chute, and as it came out of its pack, it got caught in my main chute and began wrapping itself around my legs like a cocoon.

I was now plunging head-down towards the earth. I knew with complete certainty that this was it. I was dead. This was the end of my life. When I hit the ground I wasn't going to feel anything. It would just be over. The thought did not panic me; I simply accepted it.

And I accepted something else. For the first time in my life, I felt totally helpless.

There was no way I could survive what was about to happen to me. I was no longer my own independent, self-sufficient person, in control of everything, and I never had been. The habit of my spiritual indifference had been my excuse for wanting to live as I pleased. And now I was going to die.

I heard myself say aloud, 'Oh, God, help me.' It wasn't a plea for survival. It was a plea for forgiveness. I closed my eyes and waited. I was ready to meet Him.

There was no pain; it happened so fast. Just a terrific thud, and I was lying flat on my back as though I were in bed. All of me – my head, neck, back, the back of my legs – all had landed at the same instant. I was conscious. I opened my eyes and I couldn't believe it.

I was alive. I had fallen 3600 feet from an aeroplane, and I was alive. I was lying in an irrigation ditch about eight feet deep and ten feet wide with about four inches of water in it. The softness of the mud and the water had obviously cushioned the impact of my landing.

I tried to get up, but I couldn't because my right leg was broken. I managed to take off my helmet and reserve chute pack.

I lay there for twenty minutes. No one was in a hurry to come and pick up the pieces they expected to find. The first to reach me was Paul, our instructor. He looked down at me as though he couldn't believe his eyes. 'Mark?' he asked.

'Yes, Paul, I'm okay,' I said.

I was taken by ambulance to Martin Memorial Hospital in Stuart. I broke the femur in my right leg and damaged my liver. I spent nineteen days in the hospital. My muscles, my entire body are still in the process of recovering from the shock and battering they took.

If I had landed anywhere else in that whole area – on the ground, in a tree, on any hard object or surface – I would not be here today. For this I thank God.

And I thank Him for something else. I know now that I need God, whether I am falling from an aeroplane or looking for a job or just crossing a busy street. I no longer have a habit of prayer; I have a need for prayer, whether I am asking for a blessing or thanking God for one. Every day I thank God not just for saving my life, but for bringing my faith to life. It has made my life worth living.

THE MAN WITH BIG EARS

by Linda Neukrug

When you're young, it's not what's on the inside that matters,
it's what you look like on the outside.

Alone in the hospital room, staring into the mirror, I slowly drew
a long imaginary line up and down the left side of my chest. 'Please
God,' I whispered, 'don't let my scar look too bad.' I was scheduled
for open heart surgery the next day, and do you know what scared
me? I was worried about what the scar would look like. That might
seem odd, but when you're seventeen and very self-conscious, it
is not what's going on inside that you care about, it's what you look
like on the outside. All through school I had hated gym. I especially hated the ugly old blue gym suits we'd had to wear, with
their drooping V necks and armholes far too wide. Now I pictured
hordes of classmates, whispering and pointing in the locker room:
'Look at her big, ugly scar.' And it would be ugly, I knew. I still
had scars from roller-skating falls I'd taken as a child. Keloids, the
doctor called them – raised, long-lasting scars.

Imagine what a horrible scar heart surgery will leave, I thought.

Draped in a huge hospital gown, I was shown around the floor
by the nurse. My room was in the children's section: 'Yoshiko has
leukemia. Little John there whizzing by in the wheelchair, he'll
never walk again – a car accident.' Back in my room I gave myself
a stern talking to.

'All this tragedy, and you're worrying about a scar? Forget it!
Besides, maybe it won't be as bad as you think.'

That was when a chubby blond boy of about four came trundling into my room. Climbing up on the foot of the extra bed, he gave me a suspicious once-over. 'They told me there was a grown-up here,' he said. 'My name's Calvin. What are you here for?'

'Open heart surgery.'

His little mouth dropped open. 'Me too! Me too! That's what I had!' In his excitement he bounced up and down on the bed. Then, lifting the little white undershirt he wore, he cried, 'Look! Look at my zipper! The doctor fixed me up better than new!'

Horrified, I stared. Starting below his neck and continuing down almost to his belly button, his 'zipper' was a scar probably six inches long. But to me it seemed miles long – a big ugly snake running up and down Calvin's chest.

'Mike down the hall has one, also,' he announced happily. 'And Loretta. And you'll have one, too!' He giggled, his chubby fists pounding the mattress as if it was the most wonderful joke in the world. I felt as if I couldn't breathe.

When he finally left, I snapped the light off. Maybe it was the darkness that enabled me to be fully honest. 'This sounds terrible, God, but if seeing Calvin was supposed to make me feel better, I'm sorry, but it doesn't. I feel worse! You see, I know I should be grateful that I'm going to be fine, and I know I'm being babyish about this scar – but I still don't want it!' I started to cry.

Just then I heard a tentative knock on the door. A doctor stood there, homely and stern-looking. I had never seen him before. 'What's your name?' I asked.

He flashed a broad smile and to my surprise flipped back the lapel of his white coat to display a Snoopy pin the size of a saucer. Across the bottom was a piece of adhesive tape with 'Dr Snoopy' written in bold black letters.

'Some of my patients call me Doctor Snoopy,' he said.

I told myself I would never call him that. Clearly that name was for the kids.

The doctor took a blood sample, making silly jokes so it didn't hurt too badly.

'Yours will be a pretty simple operation, as open-heart operations go,' he said. 'Do you have any questions?'

Ask him how bad the scar will be! I told myself. But I was afraid
to know. 'No questions,' I said.

'Then do you mind if I ask you one?'

'Of course not,' I said, surprised.

'Were you praying as I came in?'

His manner was so comforting that I nodded and spilled out all
the worries that I'd kept bottled up inside, everything – Calvin, the
scar. But just as I began to tell him about the gym suit, a nurse
came in. 'Doctor – er – Snoopy,' she said, 'you have a phone call.'

He got up, but before he left, he leaned over me and whispered
urgently, 'A situation may not change, but a person always can.'
He tugged at his earlobes. 'See these funny ears?' I couldn't have
missed them – they were very big. 'The kids at school used to call
me "Snoopy". It hurt my feelings. I prayed to God to change my
ears. Well, He didn't change them – but He changed me. Know
what I'd say if I met one of those old bullies now?'

'What?'

'I'd say, "It's Doctor Snoopy to you, fella!" You see, God changed
what was between my ears, inside my head.' He continued, 'God
doesn't want you to spend your life worrying about what you look
like. And about your scar – '

The nurse called again, interrupting him. 'Doctor Snoopy! Phone
call!'

'Okay, okay.' He winked and tugged at his earlobes as a part-
ing gesture.

After he left, I thought a lot about what he'd said. Then I prayed
again. But this time it was not 'God, don't let there be a scar.'
Instead, I prayed, 'Please God, change me inside. Make me less
self-conscious, less worried about what I'll look like.' For the first
time, I was able to be thankful that I would be all right. My mind
at peace, I fell asleep.

But sometimes God changes things in ways we never dream
of ...

As soon as I awoke after the operation, I peeked inside my hospital gown. 'Doctor! Doctor!' I cried. As it happened, Dr Snoopy was just entering the room to check on me. I pelted him with questions. 'Didn't you do the operation? Why is my bandage going the wrong way – across instead of up and down? Where is my zipper?'

'Of course we did the operation.' He sounded amused. 'But we deliberately made the scar go across your chest.'

'You mean I'll be able to wear my gym suit?'

He touched my forehead lightly – probably checking to see if I had a fever. I'm sure he thought I was delirious.

'A gym suit!' He said the words with all the scorn that the ugly blue article of clothing deserved. 'With my famous horizontal zipper, you can wear a gown, a bathing suit – anything you like.'

'Thank you, Doctor … Snoopy,' I whispered.

And with a big smile and one last tug on his ears, he was gone.

A TIME FOR COMPASSION

by Jacquelyn Bengter

A time for facing harsh reality and a time for tenderness.

The sky was a perfect blue as I drove along with my thirty-six-year-old brother, Hilton, who was coming home to have dinner with me and my family. After several years working as a painter and decorator, and doing some part-time modelling, he had recently moved back to live near us. Ever since returning he'd seemed quieter than usual.

'Jacquelyn,' he said. 'I have something to tell you. I had this blood test. It came back positive. I have AIDS.'

And just like that my whole world went dark. I held onto the steering wheel, feeling a blast of shock hit my chest. Oh, God! Oh, dear God! 'How long have you had it?' My voice was calm, amazingly calm, as if it belonged to someone else.

'A while now. That's why I've come home. I want to be with my family.'

'I'm glad you did,' I answered. And I was, I really was. But there was also this odd strain in my voice, a tautness of fear I hoped he didn't hear. Along with concern for Hilton, my mind was flooded with thoughts. What would this do to Mother and Daddy? How would my husband, Robert, and our four daughters react?

We had known about Hilton's homosexuality for several years. There had been a lot of pain and bitterness over it. I'd made an attempt to accept Hilton despite his lifestyle, but it was hard. Now he had AIDS. How did such things happen to nice, middle-class, church-going families?

Part of me wanted to park the car and scream. Another part wanted to reach over and hug Hilton to me, like I had done when he was a little boy. Once long ago we had been close. I remembered how I used to walk him across the street to the goldfish pond in our neighbour's front garden. I could still see him perched at the edge of the water, watching for the flash of a goldfish beneath the surface.

At that goldfish pond, Hilton and I shared a tender, unspoiled love in a place that now seemed too far away to ever have been real. As a matter of fact, Robert and I had bought that neighbour's property some time ago and rented it out. The goldfish pond had long been covered over, almost as if it had never been there …

As the memory faded, I looked at Hilton. 'We'll get through this,' I told him.

He tossed me a lopsided grin. 'Sure we will,' he said.

But I had a hard time even getting through dinner that evening. I decided not to tell Robert about it right away. I needed a little time to get used to the whole thing.

A couple of months later Hilton got sick. He still hadn't told our parents. Mum and I went with him to the doctor. I think he dreaded that almost as much as he did the disease, so I tried to prepare Mum a little, while we sat in the physician's waiting room. 'Hilton could be worse than we think,' I said. 'He hasn't really been well since coming home.'

She'd seen the ominous red spots appear on Hilton's face, the weight loss, the way the slightest cold put him flat on his back.

'The doctor wants to see you both,' a nurse interrupted. As Mum and I sat across the desk from him, I reached for her hand. 'I'm afraid Hilton has AIDS,' the doctor said. The door opened and Hilton walked in. The doctor kept talking. 'He could live another month, or two or three years. It's hard to say.'

Hilton gazed at us, tears glistening in his eyes. Mum and I got up and wrapped our arms around him. The three of us stood there entwined in that terrible knot of agony and wept.

That night, after Robert and I were in bed, I drew a deep breath. 'Hilton has AIDS,' I said. Robert was so quiet I looked over to see if he'd heard me.

'I'm sorry about Hilton,' he said finally, 'but I don't want him coming around here. We have to think about our own family.'

I sank back on my pillow. 'But he's my brother.'

Robert's face turned stony. 'I'm telling you, he's not coming here! And I don't want you having any contact with him!'

I fell silent. This was not Robert talking, was it? It sounded more like fear, pure fear.

The truth was, I understood Robert's fear only too well. I was scared too. Afraid of somehow getting the disease, afraid of how people would treat us, afraid of the stigma. Just recently, not fifty miles from here, people burned down the house of a family whose child had AIDS. Secretly I wondered if Robert was right.

My eyes wandered across the room to a picture that had been painted by a prison inmate we knew from working in a prison ministry. It was the face of Jesus. I studied it, trying to imagine Him turning away from Hilton – or from anyone who had AIDS. In a way they seemed a lot like the lepers people shunned in Bible times. Yet hadn't Jesus touched and welcomed them?

I squeezed my eyes shut. 'All right, God, I'm willing to reach out to my brother. But I need courage. I need you to soften Robert's heart along with mine. I'm turning this whole thing over to you.'

I can't explain it exactly, but the most wonderful peace wrapped around me. I waited. Days passed, then weeks. I kept up with Hilton through Mum. One morning on the phone she told me how he was painting houses, but that a lot of the time he was too sick to work. He barely had any money and could no longer afford the rent on his flat.

As I hung up, a thought popped into my head. The people who'd lived in our rented house had just left, and it was standing empty, right across the street from Mum. That evening I asked Robert, 'Couldn't we let Hilton live in our rental house?'

The lines softened in my husband's face. 'All right,' he said.

Hilton was so grateful. 'I'll paint it up like new for you,' he said over the phone. He was so happy to hear from me again his voice was chirping like a bird.

When I visited Mum, I caught glimpses of Hilton up on a ladder giving the house a fresh white coat. I even spotted him digging and planting out in the yard.

Before long my brother was visiting our house again.

One summer day I dropped in on Hilton. His eyes were beaming. 'Follow me,' he said. I trailed after him. There gleaming in the sun was the goldfish pond, same as it had been when we were small.

'Why, Hilton, it's beautiful,' I gasped. He'd dug up that small oasis where the two of us had spent so many moments together and surrounded it with flowers. Beneath the water I could see the ripple of golden fins. In his own symbolic way Hilton was trying to restore what every human heart seeks, especially in times of suffering – a circle of love and acceptance.

He squatted at the edge watching the fish, just as he'd done as a little boy. As we stood staring at the little pond, love for my brother poured through me. I put my hand on his shoulder. He looked up at me and smiled. Flecks of sunlight danced on the surface of the pond. And it seemed a new light danced inside me too.

During the following months Hilton and I grew closer than I would have dreamed possible. He came to dinner at my house weekly. Other times I cooked vegetables and took them to him, making sure he was eating properly. Sometimes we visited the goldfish pond, laughing and reminiscing. Often we sat at the kitchen table and talked. One day he looked at me and I noticed a tremble in his chin. 'When the time comes for me to die, will you be there?' he asked.

I swallowed, feeling as if my heart would break in two. 'Yes, Hilton, I'll be there,' I told him.

Each month I took him to the hospital to get his AIDS medication, AZT. One day as we sat in a waiting room full of AIDS patients, I looked around and noticed that Hilton was the only patient accompanied by a family member. Most had arrived in taxis and would leave in taxis. Alone.

The thought saddened me. Was there anyone to cook them vegetables or share healing moments beside a goldfish pond or hold their hands when it came time to die? Suddenly I felt God widening the new love that had ignited in me. I looked at the faces in that room and knew they were my brothers too, just like Hilton.

That Christmas I gave Hilton a Bible. It was nearly always beside his bed. I noticed how he had been marking passages as he read. I wanted Hilton to know God's love and peace. We talked about God's love – how it was unconditional. 'God loves us because we're His children, full stop,' I told Hilton.

By the time his second summer with AIDS came around, Hilton had been in and out of the hospital twenty times. I can't tell you how many of those times Mum and I had to get on either side of Hilton and literally carry him into the emergency room. Many people were kind to Hilton, some were not. Once Hilton was left sitting in a metal chair in the hospital corridor for hours, hardly able to hold up his head. 'Could you please find a place for him to lie down?' I begged.

'Isn't he the one with AIDS? We'll get to him when we have time,' a woman snapped.

Whenever rejection and scorn for Hilton surfaced I desperately wanted to tell people, 'I know being around him is uncomfortable for you. It was uncomfortable for me too. But don't you see? He's a real person. He's my brother. And in a way, he's your brother too.'

In the wee hours of an August morning the ringing phone startled me awake. 'Come quickly,' Mum said. 'It's Hilton.' Driving through the darkness, I kept thinking of the question Hilton once asked me: 'When the time comes for me to die, will you be there?' I pressed on the accelerator.

Hilton was barely conscious. His breathing was laboured and there was a blueness in his hands and feet. A hospice volunteer stood by his bed. I bent next to him and took his hand. 'Hilton, it's Jacquelyn. Do you know I'm here?'

His voice was a whisper. 'Yes.'

'And do you know I love you?'

His eyes grew moist and bright for a moment. 'Yes, I know,' he said. 'I love you too.' Then my brother closed his eyes. In the stillness of dawn he died.

Today when I think of Hilton and the terrible disease AIDS, I am aware of how hard it is to find our way to the deeper meaning of love. And to create a circle of acceptance big enough to take in our suffering brothers and sisters. I had to come to terms with my own fears and prejudice. And I learned that no matter how alienated we are from one another, no matter whether we agree with another's lifestyle, no matter how afraid we are, it is always more blessed to love than to fear.

FLIGHT THROUGH FEAR

by Jerrie Mock

She was going where no woman had ever gone before.

In any crisis there is a hidden danger which can be far more than the obvious one. That danger is panic, blind unreasonable panic. I found out about it in 1964, alone at the controls of an aeroplane high above the Sahara.

A rather inexperienced pilot I was trying to become the first woman to fly solo around the world. It all started when my husband Russ bought half-ownership of a single-engine Cessna 180. I think I talked Russ into that particular plane because of the loud roar of its powerful engine and the stories I'd heard about how a 180 take off with anything you could close the door on. Its Aviation Administration registration number was N1538C. When talking to the control tower, we had to say 'three-eight-Charlie' so often that the plane soon became known as 'Charlie'.

As a little girl I had greatly admired Amelia Earhart and I told my friends that someday I'd fly an aeroplane around the world. Shortly after getting Charlie I learned that no woman had ever finished what Earhart had attempted and I remembered my childhood dream. Now and then I had terrifying dreams of things like storms over the oceans, but I gradually felt certain that I should make the attempt.

Russ thought it was a great idea. The other half-owner agreed to be brave and let me risk his share of the aircraft. So, after a year of preparation, including finding sponsors, getting an instrument rating and talking Grandma into baby-sitting my two teenage boys and three-year-old daughter, Charlie and I were ready to begin our journey.

On a cold March nineteenth, Charlie roared off from the airport – with me at the controls. The cabin was practically filled by two aluminium gas tanks which left just enough room for me.

Thirteen days later we had passed over Bermuda, the Azores, Morocco and Algeria. Now I was heading for Tripoli. As Charlie's 225-horsepower engine roared on reassuringly, we climbed over the Atlas Mountains and left the blue Mediterranean behind. Bright morning sunshine splashed over the terraced green vineyards on the mountain slopes below.

I discovered that I had accidentally kicked the switch that unreeled the long-range communications radio antenna, a hundred-foot metal line that trailed behind the plane. I switched on the electric motor to reel it in.

Soon all traces of civilisation vanished and were replaced by the grim desolation of the Sahara.

I thought of camel caravans and romantic desert sheikhs. But as the desert became more stark, the loneliness of it began to get to me. I shuddered, remembering the World War II bomber, the Lady Be Good, that made a forced landing in the Libyan desert. No one ever knew what had happened to her or her crew until someone stumbled across the remains of the plane twenty-five years later.

Suddenly smoke stung my nostrils. The acrid odour of burning insulation filled the cabin. The electric motor reeling in the antenna! The limit switch hadn't turned it off!

My hand found the switch to stop the motor from grinding away at a taut wire. But it was already burning – just inches away from the giant tank filled with high-octane gasoline and explosive fumes! The motor was hidden behind the tank and I couldn't even see what was happening.

Panic flooded through me. How much heat could that thin aluminium skin absorb? The smoke thickened. Any second I knew we could explode into a white ball of flame to be scattered in fragments over the craggy area below. No one would ever know.

My hands froze on the controls. I had no parachute. What should I do? What could I do?

Do something! Do anything!

Land the plane! Impulsively I reached for the throttle to slacken power for a landing. No, I'd surely crash in the rocks and sand or trigger an explosion.

Reason told me to sit quietly. But panic paralyses the powers of reason. And now my mind flapped like a frightened bird caught in a net. Crazy fears flew at me, wild ideas about landing the plane stormed my mind.

I told myself to relax. I couldn't. Instinctively I reached for something to grasp – something with which I could steady myself. And then I thought of the psalm I had learned as a child. I spoke the words haltingly.

'The Lord is my shepherd. I have everything I need … He lets me rest in fields of green grass … He gives me new strength.'

As I repeated the comforting words, the wild fears subsided and a calm peace began to fill me.

And then – I can't say how long it took, probably a few minutes though it seemed like hours – the smell of burning wire and insulation went away. After consuming the insulation on the wires, the fire had burned itself out. The air in the cabin cleared.

Charlie churned along as smoothly as ever; I was still an explorer out to see a glorious, untamed world.

I breathed a grateful prayer of thanks, not so much for saving me from a fiery death but for saving me from panic. For, as it turned out, panic was the real danger; it could have precipitated me into disaster through some crazy, unreasonable act. Panic has caused so many tragedies that could have been averted in those first critical seconds if someone had just stayed calm enough to judge the situation correctly.

When an emergency arises, whether it be at the controls of an aeroplane or when facing a crisis of another sort, I have learned to take a deep breath and stand steady rather than run blindly. For I know that when I rest in God, I will emerge from the dark cloud with wings level, safe on course.

LITTLE WORRIES

by Robert Baker

Remembering you were small once.

When our youngest daughter, Rebecca was only six years old, a destructive storm passed through our community tearing up trees and destroying houses. Our home was not directly involved, yet it was so close that it frightened us all, and left a deep impression upon Rebecca.

Later, when it stormed and the wind rippled the tiles on the roof above her bedroom upstairs, Rebecca sometimes recalled the earlier experience and was alarmed.

One night, when I went up to comfort her, I pointed out that the chances for such a bad storm to hit our area again was most remote.

I had knelt beside her bed as I talked, and when I was done, she reached up, put her arms around my neck, drew me down close and whispered, 'Yes, Dad, but you don't know what it's like to be little.'

As an adult, I sometimes forget what it is like to be little, physically or spiritually. Too often I attempt to laugh off the fears of others, when instead they need my comfort, my simple statement, 'I understand, I care, your concern is my concern, your fear is my fear.'

Today when I talk to others, I try not to forget that once I was little – and sometimes still am.

TRUE GRIT

by John Wayne

The Hollywood actor learns what courage really means.

Long before I ever made the movie *True Grit,* people would talk about my screen characters in terms of courage, firmness, stamina – true grit. But what about the man who played those characters?

Certainly I have never thought of myself as a timid type. Even as a child I know I had a certain brashness. I remember two incidents in particular when I was a little boy and my family was staying in the Mojave Desert. The four of us – my mother, father, younger brother and I – had come from a little town in Iowa where dad had been a pharmacist, but because of his health the doctors had told him he should move west. At first he had thought about going to Montana, but my grandfather wrote and said, 'Why not come to California and starve?' We did both.

Dad found some isolated land in Antelope Valley, not close to anything, yet not too far from Lancaster. He built a house for us which was hardly more than a shack and he tried to grow corn on the land as though we were back in Iowa, which clearly we were not. We had a pretty desperate time of it. I was hardly aware of it, because I was happy – especially, I recall, because I had my own horse which I took care of and rode back and forth to school. Her name was Jenny, and I loved her.

One Halloween night out there in the desert, my brother, Bob, and I had just come to the table when my mum brought out a bowl full of weenies, a type of meatball, a special treat since we didn't have meat very often. Just at that moment we all heard an eerie sound.

'Who-o-o-o. Who-o-o-o-o.'

It was my dad standing outside the screen door with a sheet over his head, but I thought it was the bogey man. I grabbed the bowl of weenies and flung it at the apparition. It broke up dad's performance.

As I look back, hurling that bowl of weenies at the bogey man came as natural to me as a knee jerk. Not too long after that, though, I was asked to do something that required a different kind of courage. My horse, Jenny, began to get so thin that people in town accused me of not feeding her. Finally the vet told us that for her own good we should destroy her – which was like destroying me. I didn't want to do it, but it had to be done. So it was done.

Those things were way back in my childhood, but years later, in the Autumn of 1964, I came face to face with a different kind of demand: the big C. In October I had gone down to the Scripps Clinic in La Jolla for my very belated yearly check-up. I knew I had been coughing a lot more, but I wasn't in any kind of pain.

The doctors kept taking X rays, and I was getting impatient. When they sent me back for the fourth set of pictures, I said to the X-ray doctor, 'What's the deal?'

'Well, it's positive, of course, but beyond – '

'Wait a minute. Positive? What are you telling me?'

'I'm sorry,' the doctor said, 'didn't you know?'

When I left the clinic that day, I realised I must have a lung operation as fast as possible and that there were a lot of arrangements to make, but for the moment I was dazed. I had promised Senator Goldwater, who was running for president then, that I would appear at a rally in San Diego, and I headed there. I sat in the back of the audience instead of on the stage. I don't know why. I wasn't trying to escape attention; I think I just wanted to be close to people.

Before the end of the rally, they had hauled me up on the stage and the crowd cheered and I remember thinking how odd it would be if they knew what was happening, that I was standing there a bewildered man in the first flush of fear.

I'm a big man physically and I was lucky to have been born with an unusual amount of strength and stamina. All my life I've been grateful for those physical gifts. They shaped my career. They made it possible for me to play football for the Southern Cal Trojans, which led directly to my getting a summer job as a prop man with a movie studio; and a bit of muscle wasn't exactly a hindrance for the rest of my career in pictures either. But any dim-witted thug knows that physical strength is not the same as courage. And that night in San Diego, I needed courage.

Obviously, there was no bludgeoning one's way out of this one; there was nothing to hurl at the bogey man. My very helplessness gave me awful twinges of fear. Mark Twain wasn't being humorous when he wrote that, 'Courage is resistance to fear, mastery of fear – not absence of fear.' If I was going to do battle with cancer bravely, I knew what it was that I had to conquer first.

In this struggle I had a lot of allies – my family and friends, of course. And prayer. I did a lot of praying in those few shaky days before the operation, and this I know: There is a Man Upstairs holding all this world together, including you and me. You cannot believe this, and believe it firmly, without drawing the strength, the courage, to master your fears.

The operation was successful, thank God. They cut away a lung, but they left me alive and grateful, and ready to learn something more about adversity. Overcoming trouble can be like skidding in a car on a slippery road. There's the first skid which, if you can control it, you feel pretty relieved about. But there is an after-skid waiting to surprise you from the other direction. My after-skid was getting back in harness again.

With all that vaunted energy of mine, I was surprised at how much the operation had slowed me up. I began to think about it, and worry. My conscience hurt me because I had been scheduled to make a picture with Dean Martin called *The Sons of Katie Elder*. Everybody had been most considerate about the postponement, but now time was wasting, careers were being interfered with, money was going down the drain. Finally I made up my mind to do the picture but I had misgivings about myself, about my strength. Those reservations were taken care of by that tremendous old director, Henry Hathaway.

Hathaway had directed me in a number of films, and luckily he had the assignment on *Katie Elder*. It was he, really, who got me going again, though not with tender loving care. That man was merciless. The film was shot on location in Durango, Mexico, which is 8000 feet above sea level, not the best place for breathing even with two lungs. It didn't take me long to figure out what Hathaway was up to. He was being deliberately tough on me. He had me getting soaked in the river, jumping out of boats hand-cuffed, always testing me. I was determined not to let him get the best of me.

One evening we had a night shoot in which I was supposed to come riding down a street on a horse carrying a rocking chair in one hand, a Bible in the other and a basket over one arm. I was supposed to stop, dismount and walk into a girl's house. The horse I was riding had never worked at night before and he was fractious and hard to handle. I kept doing the scene over and over, mounting, dismounting and mounting again with all those encumbrances. Hathaway watched me carefully, but no more carefully than I was watching myself, for I was getting tired. At last when he finally called out, 'Print it! Let's go to bed,' I knew for sure that not only had I beaten Hathaway at his game, but that I had also won my fight with cancer.

Why had Hathaway chosen to take such a rough tack with me? Why did I let him? Because, more than ten years before, he had undergone an operation for cancer far worse than mine. He knew me well. He knew just how far he could push me and he used the courage he had shown in his own recovery to help bring about mine. Nowadays it's one of the rewards for me that I am able to tell people that simply because they have cancer doesn't mean they're at the end of the road.

It is good and it is helpful to have physical strength; but looking back, I am certain that the truest part of true grit is not physical – it's moral. It is something really tough, something we all fail at from time to time. It is making a decision and standing firm in it, whether it's submitting to an operation or putting an ailing pet to sleep. It is doing what must be done. After all, if you think about it, that's the root of all morality, for no moral man can have peace of mind if he leaves undone what he knows he should have done.

The movies' all-time top box office attraction, John Wayne has appeared in more than 200 films. A 1932 film, *Ride Him, Cowboy,* was followed almost forty years later by *True Grit* which earned Wayne an Oscar. His wife, Pilar, is the proud mother of his seven children and grandmother to his nineteen grandchildren.

FEAR OF FIRE

by an unknown reporter

A man's greatest fear is overcome.

A man lay trapped inside the cab of a smouldering fourteen-wheel trailer, which had rammed into a tree. His truck had been forced off the road by a drunken driver.

Police officer Don Henry, responding to a radio SOS, raced to the scene. A recovery vehicle pulled up. But even after towlines had been attached to the cab door, the crushed metal refused to budge.

Someone screamed, 'Look. Fire!' Flames began to flicker from the bottom of the cab. In a few minutes, the truck would be a funeral pyre.

Then out of the night strode a towering figure. 'Can I be of any help?' He spoke softly. 'We've done all we can,' replied Henry. 'They've gone for cutting torches. It's our last hope.'

The stranger paused only a second, then walked up to the cab and slowly wrenched off the jammed door with his bare hands.

'You could hear the metal rip,' said Henry later. 'I saw the big man's shirt sleeves split open as his tremendous muscles bulged.'

The truck driver was alive but unconscious when Henry hauled him to safety. But when Henry looked for the giant rescuer, he had disappeared into the night. 'Who was the mysterious Samson?' the local newspapers asked the next morning. For days the question went unanswered. Then the foreman of a local transport company noticed that a thirty-three-year-old named Charles Jones had strange cuts on his hands and moved away from crowds that talked about the accident.

Jones, it turned out, was the modern Samson. 'God gives one strength to do anything in an emergency,' he said when questioned.

What Jones did not say was that for the past fourteen months he had been terribly afraid of fire – ever since his own child died in the flames of their burning home.

HOW I LEARNED TO LIVE WITH A LIZARD

by Helen Erskine

One creature helps another.

There were about twenty-five women in the public speaking course I took, each one feeling she had a different reason for being there. But, whether we admitted it or not, the underlying purpose of us all was to learn how to overcome fear – in our case, stage fright at facing an audience.

During one session the instructor casually announced that we were to give an impromptu talk on how each of us had overcome some other fear. At the start we were petrified. It was then, in our extremity, we discovered we all had something to say. During this session many of us, in our soul-searching, revealed hidden fears which we probably never had admitted even to ourselves.

The inspiration for my impromptu talk came from the two women who preceded me. One had said, 'Conquer fear by facing it'. The other happened to mention a lizard. Suddenly, my subconscious handed me the topic of my speech: 'The Time I Learned to Live With a Lizard.'

In May 1953, I had gone as a magazine correspondent to cover the tour of a political leader to the Middle East and Asia. The schedule was tough: Thirteen countries in twenty days. Our flight over the Arabian Sea proved pleasant and uneventful. We landed at Karachi as the sun rose. At the hotel my bearer or servant – an elderly, white-turbanned Muslim with a muff-like beard and friendly eyes – conducted me to a high-ceilinged room, deposited my luggage, and bowed out.

I was told that this manservant was never to leave my presence and was to guard me as long as I stayed. He settled on a mat outside my door.

Hoping to snatch a couple of hours' sleep before the day really began, I slipped into bed. It was cool and quiet. I had all but dozed off when a breeze, rattling the blinds, awakened me. It was then, for the first time, I became aware of a creature moving on the wall opposite my bed. Terror-stricken, I looked again. A large lizard with a vivid green back and yellow belly was regarding me intently.

I have a genuine horror of lizards or any other crawling reptile. To me they are loathsome. I've tried to overcome this because I love animals. Horses, dogs, cats, even white mice have been my adored pets, complicating my life ever since I was born, and I wouldn't want it otherwise.

I'll go all out for any animal. I once sat in the middle of a road, holding the head of a dying cab horse in my lap. He had been struck by a hit-and-run driver, and the policeman in charge wouldn't shoot him till the owner gave his consent. It took the owner an hour to reach where the horse and I, surrounded by curious crowds, waited. Remembering the look of trust in that old horse's eyes, I have never been so sorry. In his pain he might have bitten me, but he didn't and I wasn't afraid.

Yet here I was – terrified by a lizard, in reality only a few inches long! Remembering St Francis of Assisi and his love for all living things, I tried to tell myself that this lizard in Karachi was just as much a creature of God as that horse in the road, but it did no good. I lay there absolutely petrified. Meanwhile, the lizard continued to stare unblinkingly at me with its cold, beady, black eyes. Occasionally its long pink tongue ribboned out tentatively. What was I to do?

Finally I forced myself to act. With trembling hands, I slipped on my dressing gown and tiptoed to the door, fearful every step of the way that the lizard might give chase. Screaming, 'There's a lizard in my room!' I flung open the door.

The bearer, curled on a mat outside, looked up in astonishment. 'But madam, there is a lizard in every room.'

'I am afraid of lizards. Kill it; take it away; do something to get it out of my room at once.'

The bearer got to his feet. 'If I do remove this lizard, madam, you will be plagued by all manner of insects – flies, mosquitoes, bugs. Learn to live with him. He is your friend. Once you realise this, your fear will vanish.'

Ashamed of my fear, I forced myself to go back into the room. The lizard was still on the wall. The idea of sleeping in the same room with this repulsive-looking thing almost finished me. After all I had faced and been through in my life, did I have to take this? Goodness knows what other queer, reptilian company it might attract. Then, once again, I thought of St Francis of Assisi who loved all living creatures, no matter whether they walked on two or four feet, or crawled. In his eyes lizards were just as much a part of God's creation as we. So, though consumed by fear, I went to bed thinking of St Francis. It was a long while before I fell asleep. When I awoke, the lizard was still on the opposite wall. That evening, the bearer, anxious to reassure me, suggested I bring a little sugar from the restaurant. He thought if I approached the lizard gently, it might take a few grains of the sugar on its tongue. The first attempt was as frightening to the lizard as to me. He raced up the wall to the ceiling and stayed there. The third day he accepted my offer of sugar. By the time I left, we were really friends. I no more feared him than he me. The poor little creature had a job to do just like the rest of us – he was just part of the plan.

THE ROCK

by Barbara Fairchild

This singer discovered a new song.

Most entertainers spend thousands of hours on the road. It's part of the job. The likelihood of accidents is a possibility that we live with on a daily basis. For me, that possibility became a reality one day in the mountains of Colorado.

I have been a singer nearly all my life. I entered my first talent show when I was five years old. Music was the rock that saw me through hard times and good times.

I wish I could say church was as important to me, but it wasn't. I was raised in St Louis, in a strictly religious home, with emphasis on the strict. It seemed to me that nobody ever talked about loving God, just about following the rules.

As I got older and my rebellion became more noticeable, the list of things I couldn't do got longer. One night Mum insisted I make a choice: I could live my life right or plan on going to hell. At the time, my own desires seemed more real to me than hell did. I moved out and quit going to church.

To all appearances, things went well. I was able to make a living by singing. Often, driving to club dates, I found myself thinking. I was on the road a lot. What if I had an accident? I was afraid of dying and I didn't want to go to hell, so I vowed to be extra careful on the roads.

Soon the focus of my career moved to Nashville. Often when I was there I stayed with a girlfriend of mine named Peggy, also a singer. She was one of those people who always smiled. Unless you knew her, you couldn't tell how terrible her life was. But this time she was so happy that I finally said, 'What on earth has happened to you? I've never seen you so happy.'

She said, 'I got saved.'

Now in my old church we never talked about being saved, so I said, 'Really, where? From what?' So she started talking about God and how He had changed her life. She was going to church that night and she asked me to go along. I didn't have anything else to do, so I went. Before that week was out, Jesus invaded my life. I fell in love with Him and gave my life to Him.

My life changed. I quit singing and became totally immersed in church activities to the exclusion of everything else.

Finally one day my husband said, 'I'm just going to tell you one thing. Then I'm not going to bring it up anymore. If you think that God saved you so you could sit here on your behind and say "Glory, hallelujah, I'm going to heaven when I die", then you'd better think again. If every time a person becomes a Christian, he or she refuses to go where the people don't know about God, who's going to tell them?

'You know, Barbara, when I first met you, you were the sweetest person I'd ever known. But since you got religion you're the most selfish wretch I've ever seen. Why don't you start thinking about the people who need to hear what you sing?'

Well! That got me thinking, I'll tell you. The upshot was that I went back to singing.

But that meant I had to start travelling again. Shortly thereafter, I recorded 'The Teddy Bear Song' – and watched, amazed, as it became a number one hit. Suddenly my concerts were in great demand, and our schedule necessitated that my band and I hit the road in a bus.

The bus was convenient, and even pleasant. We each had a bunk, and there was a television and a tape player to pass the time. I even brought along a mini-sewing machine. Things went well – until one fateful day.

It was late when we boarded the bus after the concert the night before. We had been doing a series of concerts throughout Colorado. To reach our next destination in time to perform, we'd have to drive straight through without stopping. To do so, our professional driver had trained John, one of our band members, to drive the bus so the two of them could share the driving.

That night, I was bone tired and ready to sack out. As we started our ascent into the mountains, I managed to kick off my shoes before snuggling into the cocoon-warmth of my bunk in the back of the bus. Within moments I was asleep.

After several hours, the driver pulled over and woke John to replace him. The two of them went over the map and the route. Then we started off again.

Sometime later, John realised he must have missed the marked route. Rather than wake the driver, he looked at the map and found another road that looked possible. He didn't know that in the mountains, roads can quickly become too narrow or too steep for a bus to negotiate. That's what happened. As the climb became steeper and steeper, the bus slowed to a crawl. Finally it couldn't go any farther. We came to a stop.

I awoke to the sudden stillness of the engine being shut off. It was overheated, and the driver decided to let it cool while finding the best way out of this predicament. Most of the band members woke up and got off the bus to study the problem. There was nothing I could do to help, so I drifted back to sleep.

In a few minutes I felt the bus start to move backward. I looked out of my bunk, and there was no driver at the wheel. Keith, my piano player, stuck his head out of his bunk too. 'What's happening?' I asked.

'I'll go see,' he said, and he jumped up. The driver forgot that the bus's air brakes were run by the engine. Once the air escaped, there was nothing holding us. The bus rolled backward, picking up more and more speed. We careened off the road. There were no trees on that slope, nothing to break our fall.

I was thrown from my bunk, tossed around like a rag doll. Keith came falling back my way. The pain was excruciating as I was slammed against the walls and bunks.

But then something incredible happened. In place of terror, I felt washed with a perfect peace. This is the day I'll see heaven, I thought. From that moment I felt no pain.

The bus stopped. It was hanging onto a giant boulder by the front axle, tottering precariously. Keith and I stared at each other dumbly for a millisecond. Then we slowly and carefully started helping each other up the steep pitch of the bus aisle. When John reached the bus and climbed in to help us, his face told us we were still in danger.

When the three of us finally stood safe on solid ground, I saw how we had been stopped in the middle of nothingness. I patted that boulder, and exclaimed, 'Jesus is my rock!'

To this day, people think it is incredible that my life was saved when the bus rolled off the mountain. But the real miracle wasn't that my life was saved; it's that God did not give up on the girl who gave up on Him years before. That day He even took away my fear of death. Today, though music is still an important part of me, I know that nothing can ever take the place of the true Rock of my life.

PERIL ON THE SEA

by Muriel Marvinney

Disaster hits a holiday cruise.

It started out on the golf course last year when my good friend Agnes Lillard asked, 'Muriel, how would you like to take a cruise to the Orient?'

'You're kidding!' I said.

'No. I'm not,' Agnes replied. 'I saw an advert in the paper about a month-long cruise to Red China, Japan and Singapore. A few other places, too.'

'Sounds good to me,' I replied.

We're both widows, Agnes and I. After my husband died in 1974 we became close friends. Agnes' husband had died some years before, so it was only natural that we sought each other's company.

Our families are wonderful. We're both fortunate that our children and grandchildren (Agnes and I have five grandchildren between us) live nearby and visit us often.

But, loving as our children are, and with all the dear friends both Ag and I have, there is a kind of invisible barrier for us widows. You're always the fifth wheel at social gatherings. It's not deliberate, mind you. As Agnes says, 'After all, the world goes two by two.'

Despite that, the two of us kept busy and interested and involved, and our lives were never dull. When we broached the idea of our taking 'a slow boat to China' our children were all for it. The more I thought about it, the more exciting the idea seemed.

All summer we pored over brochures like a couple of kids. Our departure date was set for 28 September 1981.

After a round of bon voyage parties in late September, we left on schedule, flying to Vancouver, our port of embarkation.

We boarded our cruise ship, which was part of the Holland American Lines, on Tuesday, 30 September. It wasn't as large as I had thought it would be, but it was beautifully appointed. It had one of those impressive Dutch names: the *S.S. Prinsendam*.

Our fellow passengers were from all over the world, all as anxious as Ag and I to visit Red China. Almost immediately we began to make friends. There was one couple we were particularly fond of, Grace and Paul Miller, whom we met at breakfast on our first morning. They were the kind of caring people who make you feel totally at ease.

The scenery, as our ship made its way up Alaska's coastal inland waterway that first day, was gorgeous. There were towering cliffs on either side of us, and when the channel would narrow down they'd loom over us.

Thursday morning, we stopped at Ketchikan, our first port of call in Alaska. It was raining, but Ag and I went shopping. I bought my baby grandson an exquisite pair of tiny mukluks – soft, fur-lined Eskimo boots. Then the sun came out as we got underway again, and it turned out to be a gorgeous day. We played deck tennis all afternoon.

Friday found the *Prinsendam* steaming into Glacier Bay, which is part of the National Parks system. They turned the engines off and we silently drifted close to the towering walls of ice. The day was overcast, but the sun, intermittently peeking through grey banks of clouds, glanced off the blue-streaked glaciers, so that they sparkled like sapphires. It was a starkly beautiful landscape, untouched by man since creation's dawn. We felt insignificant in comparison. We felt God ...

After a while, the *Prinsendam* slowly turned around and headed out of the bay into the Gulf of Alaska. Our next port of call, nine days hence, would be Yokahama.

Friday, 3 October, we had a lovely dinner. Afterward, both Agnes and I were so tired we could hardly keep our eyes open; it had been such a full day. We retired to the cabin we shared at about midnight. I set my alarm for six o'clock.

No sooner had I laid my head on the pillow when I thought my alarm went off. Puzzled, I groped for the clock in the darkened cabin. Then I realised that the ringing bell was in the corridor. Almost simultaneously Agnes and I got up and went to the door. My hand shook as I opened it. In the confined space, the air reverberated with the clang of the bell and banging of heavy metal doors slamming shut.

A ship's officer was coming out of his cabin, directly opposite ours.

'What's going on?' Agnes asked.

The officer grabbed a sweater from his cabin and came back. 'I'd advise you two ladies to dress warmly, because I think I smell smoke,' he said. Then he disappeared through a door leading to the stairwell.

'Oh, let's just go up on deck as we are and see what's happening,' I suggested casually.

'No!' Agnes said firmly. 'Muriel, the officer said to dress warmly, and that's what we're going to do!'

We quickly dressed, putting on slacks and sweaters and light raincoats. Wisps of smoke were now seeping under our cabin door.

'Will you hurry up, Muriel?' Agnes said, as I sat trying to untie a stubborn knot in my shoelace.

'I'll have to carry it,' I said, clutching the shoe and a life jacket and limping into the companionway.

When we stepped out onto the deck, we saw only a few other people there. It was a beautiful, clear night.

'So there's a little fire somewhere,' Agnes said. 'They have all kinds of foam and chemicals to put it out. We'll be back down in our cabins in no time.'

'Sure,' I said, reassured, yet shivering slightly. My purse and my jewellery were locked in my suitcase. Well, it couldn't be helped ...

People were straggling in small groups out onto the deck now, in all stages of dress and undress.

'Why, they just opened our door with a passkey and routed us out of a sound sleep!' a woman with hair curlers was saying indignantly to a friend.

'Guess we'll have something to tell the family back home!' a fellow quipped.

The passengers seemed casual, almost festive. There was no sign of confusion or panic. They remained calm even when the captain's voice came over the loudspeaker: 'Ladies and gentlemen, we have a fire in the engine room. There is nothing to be concerned about. The fire is contained.' It was 1.30 a.m.

One of the younger women had brought her camera and began taking pictures. Some of the crew, led by the captain's wife, began passing out blankets and life jackets to those who had been caught unprepared.

Ag and I decided to return to our cabin, but when we stepped inside the stairwell, we were met by an officer wearing a gas mask, emerging from the smoke-filled stairs. He told us that there was no way we could return to our cabins. Reluctantly, we went into the theatre, which was on the Promenade Deck, to wait things out.

What a nuisance! The theatre was cold and there were no lights. It was now a little past 2 a.m.

'You know, Muriel, they'll just have to turn back to port,' Ag said. 'All of our clothes are smoke-damaged by now. I just wish they'd tell us more!'

Just then seven bells sounded. 'All passengers will report to their boat stations,' the captain's voice boomed over the speakers. 'We have lowered the lifeboats to deck level, but only as a precaution.'

Dutifully we went to our stations. As we passed the radio room, we could hear the SOS signals being tapped out by the operator. Those little blips seemed insistent, frantic.

We had had a boat drill on Wednesday – which we hadn't taken too seriously. Now I wished I had.

Then the captain's voice came over the speakers again: 'The Coast Guard is on its way with special fire fighting equipment, but we think the fire is under control.'

Agnes and I looked at each other. Thick, black smoke was billowing out of the stairwells.

Suddenly all the lights went out, except for one on the bridge. We didn't know it then, but the ship's electrical system had failed and with it the pumps fighting the fire. It was weird, drifting in that vast blackness with only the stars and the brilliant Northern Lights overhead.

Then two helicopters appeared, hovering overhead and sweeping the water with giant searchlights. A plane buzzed our ship. Thank God! Help was on the way.

Someone came running along the deck and said he had heard explosions in the aft section.

'Oh, dear God,' Agnes prayed aloud, 'please let it be daylight soon!'

A few minutes later the captain announced: 'All lifeboat commanders report to the bridge immediately.'

'Uh-oh!' I said to Agnes, feeling weak. 'This sounds serious!'

In a few minutes the commanders came down from the bridge on the run. Then I saw them – huge red flames shooting out of the lounge area. The fire was burning out of control!

'This is it, Ag!' I cried.

'ALL PASSENGERS INTO THE LIFEBOATS!' the captain's voice boomed. 'I REPEAT: ALL PASSENGERS INTO THE LIFEBOATS!'

'I don't believe this!' Agnes gasped. Suddenly people were five-deep at the railing. There was no panic, except for a bit of shoving as crew members asked us to move back so they could open the railing.

'Passengers only!' an officer said. 'Passengers only!' Two crewmen pressed forward and leaped over the railing into the lifeboat. *They're going to help us into the boat,* I thought. Instead they disappeared under blankets. I felt anger and disgust, but in a moment it melted into pity for their cowardice. We were all afraid.

The passengers pouring out of the lounge and theatre were opposite our boat station. Instead of going to their assigned stations, they crowded at ours. In a short while our boat was jammed with a mass of humanity. Agnes had a seat, but I was standing. Between us, a big, heavy-set girl was wedged. She was leaning all over Ag.

'Uh … I can't breathe,' Ag said. 'Could you … uh … move a little?'

'I can't budge!' the girl gasped. In a less perilous situation it would have been funny. But we weren't laughing.

Suddenly with a groan, the lifeboat tilted at a crazy angle, leaning towards the ship. Looking straight down, we could see the waves slapping the hull. People began screaming. There was no time to think, no time to pray! Instinctively everyone leaned in the opposite direction. The lifeboat righted itself.

'Twenty people will have to leave this boat!' an officer yelled from the deck of the *Prinsendam*. 'We have other lifeboats! Please!' There were 510 people aboard the ship; we had no idea how many lifeboats there were. But reluctantly passengers began jumping back into the ship's deck. I still didn't have a seat, but at least now we could breathe. Incredibly, there were 85 people jammed into lifeboat No. 4, in a 30-by-10-foot space.

The officers pressed the button to activate the lowering mechanism. Nothing happened – no electrical power. Now, frantically, the officers worked to lower the boats manually.

Suddenly the pulleys holding the lifeboat slipped, plunging us into the ocean in one heart-stopping drop of seventy feet. Had the boat tilted we'd have all been pitched into the sea. It struck the water hard, with a tremendous splash. My eyes locked with Ag's; we could hardly believe we were still in the boat.

Then the waves began bashing the lifeboat against the steel hull of the ship – once, twice, three times. Someone screamed.

The boat was sturdy, but how much pounding could it take before it began to crack? We were so jammed in that it was impossible to use the oars.

Dear God, I prayed, please carry us safely beyond the ship ... please!

Wham! Again we slammed the hull with a bone-jarring impact. Wham! Then, miraculously, we were clear. Thank you, God!

Now, as the space between the lifeboat and the *Prinsendam* widened, I was seized with a feeling hard to describe, a feeling of utter loneliness ... even though I was pressed in on all-sides by a mass of humanity. Although the *Prinsendam* was ablaze, it was big and stable and felt safe. But now we were adrift in the night in a little cockleshell of a lifeboat.

Luckily the sea was calm. Except for a little pencil flashlight one person had, we were in total darkness. Dimly we could make out black objects bobbing – here a rubber raft, there another lifeboat. We could hear muffled voices:

'Look out!' 'Push off there.' 'Oh, sweet Jesus.'

Silently we prayed for daylight and the help that surely was on the way. Hadn't the captain said something about a Coast Guard cutter coming for us? But how long would it take to arrive? We had to be 150 miles off the coast ...

At the helm of our thirty-foot lifeboat was the ship's second maitre d'. He did what little steering he could.

After an hour or so, somebody started singing 'Row, Row, Row Your Boat,' but in our desperate situation it fizzled. People sat mutely huddled in their blankets, with their eyes closed. I saw lips moving in silent prayer. It was getting light.

At about 10 a.m. the sea began to get rough. We had no way of knowing it, but we were heading into the tail end of a typhoon. One of the women became violently seasick. Between spasms she announced: 'If this boat capsizes, we'll survive exactly twelve minutes. The water is freezing.'

Now the temperature began to drop rapidly. I was grateful that we had dressed warmly, but my heart went out to the half-dressed people huddling under damp blankets. One woman had plastic wrap around her bare feet. Even if we had had an extra sweater or coat, there was no room to make an exchange. We were so packed together that even the meagre food supplies could not be opened and distributed.

Finally we saw smoke on the horizon. A ship! But it was so far away! A tender from the *Prinsendam* approached another crowded lifeboat. The crew of the tender tried to manoeuvre close enough to attach a line to the other boat to tow it to the ship that lay over the horizon. We held our breaths as the drama unfolded. If they could rescue them, then there would be hope for us too. But by now the ocean was so rough that the line kept snapping. They finally gave up and moved away. Our hearts sank.

It was noon now. We had been adrift six hours.

Where was the Coast Guard cutter the captain had mentioned? Why didn't the ship whose smoke we'd seen come to get us?

Now the waves were monsters: 20–25 feet high. The maitre d' struggled to keep the prow pointed into the waves. If the over-loaded boat were hit broadside by one of those giant swells, we'd capsize.

'Oh, Muriel, we'll never make it!' Ag said, clutching my hand. For the first time since our ordeal began, I began to think she was right; I knew other people must be feeling the same way.

I thought of my children, Sandy, Pam and Roger; I thought of Roger's wife. I thought of my baby grandson. I guessed I'd never see him wear his tiny mukluks. My eyes filled. Around me now, people were quiet; there was no panic, no hysteria; no one cried out.

Somehow I wasn't afraid, and I wondered why. Then I remembered: In my mind's eye I could see the hospital room where my husband, Louis, lay dying. The children and I were at his bedside, as he quietly slipped away with the fading daylight.

The months of hospitalisation had been a terrible strain on all of us, but that day, at the very end, an indescribable feeling of peace permeated the room. It wasn't merely the emotional reaction of a grieving wife; the children felt it, too. The very presence of God was in that room, uplifting us, transporting us beyond sorrow and fear. I knew then that, no matter what, I would never fear death again.

Now, in the midst of that raging sea, the memory of that special moment was a calming comfort.

'I think it would be a good idea if we prayed,' an attractive woman said in a soft southern accent.

We all bowed our heads. 'Lord God,' she prayed, 'we ask you to be with us in our hour of peril. Lord, calm this raging sea, as you calmed the waves of Galilee. Preserve us, your children. Our Father, who art in Heaven.'

From all over the boat voices joined in repeating the prayer. In spite of the babble of so many languages – English, Dutch, French, German – we were all one at that moment.

When we came to the words 'deliver us from evil', my heart thrilled. Never before had I prayed those words with such need, such faith.

A long time later we heard the mutter of a helicopter; then it was there, skimming over the ocean. It hovered over another lifeboat about a mile away. A tiny basket was lowered on what appeared to be a spider's thread.

'Hurrah!' the cry went up from everyone aboard our boat as the helicopter began lifting people one by one from the boat. When it had about fifteen people aboard, it sped off.

Another helicopter arrived and began lifting people from a rubber raft. *It won't be long now,* I thought. But we waited and waited, and the helicopters seemed not to notice us.

I had lost my brother during World War II; he had been lost in the North Sea. *Wouldn't it be ironic,* I thought, *if I went the same way?*

An exploding flare brought me out of my dismal reverie. Our 'captain', the maitre d', had fired it to get the attention of the copters. A few minutes later he fired another. One of the helicopters turned and was flying toward us …

Ninety minutes and 138 air-miles later, we touched down at the Coast Guard station at Yakutat, Alaska. It was a little after 5 p.m., Saturday, 4 October. Our ordeal in the lifeboat had lasted ten hours.

All around us were strong, gentle hands; caring hands. Those wonderful Coast Guard men. Somehow they weren't strangers. They were like fathers, brothers, sons!

They wrapped us in blankets and gave us hot coffee. I was vaguely aware of someone snapping pictures. After I had warmed up a bit, I looked at myself in a mirror; my hair was a mass of corkscrews. I didn't know whether to cry or laugh.

I got to a phone and called home.

'I'm all right,' I told Pam and Roger. 'Please call Ag's son Peter and tell him we are both okay. Tell him she'll call as soon as she can.'

'Mum, they told us they were able to save your luggage too,' Pam said brightly.

Dear Pam. How could she know what we'd been through? 'Honey,' I said, 'they got it wrong. I have only what is on my back!'

Ten minutes later they flew us to Sitka where we were given a room in a hotel. After taking long, hot baths, Agnes and I went to a lovely little shop across the street and purchased new outfits, courtesy of the Holland America Lines.

After dinner at our hotel, we retired. That first night we slept like logs. The bad nights wouldn't start until Sunday when, the minute we'd turn the lights out, it would all come rushing back. Then we'd have to turn the lights on and talk; we needed to feel the warmth of human contact, to know that we were safe and warm and would be returning to our loved ones in a day or so.

Sunday morning when we came down to breakfast, word came that twenty passengers were still missing and presumed dead. The list included our new friends Grace and Paul Miller.

Everyone was stunned. 'It can't be! It just can't!' Agnes said over and over.

We picked listlessly at our food; suddenly the cheerful dining room seemed like a tomb. Those of us who had survived needed one another. But we needed those others too.

Dearest Lord, I prayed silently, please save them too ... please.

That prayer too was answered. Later that day we learned that all of the missing were aboard a Coast Guard cutter. At about 6 p.m. we had a joyful reunion with the Millers. What a tale they had to tell! If it hadn't been for the beam of Paul Miller's £1.99 flashlight, the cutter might have missed them completely in the dark!

On Monday we left for Seattle, where we stayed overnight. On Thursday, we were flown home, where our families were waiting.

It was a tearful, joyful scene at the airport. Ag and I each wound up with two sets of T-shirts reading 'I Survived the Prinsendam'.

But we did more than survive. Agnes and I both grew from our harrowing experience on the sea. I think it had something to do with our feeling of loss and grief on hearing the reports that the Millers and eighteen others were lost. It had to do with the bond we all felt as we drifted helplessly in that lifeboat. It had to do with the courage of the US Air Force and the Coast Guard – all those brave, wonderful men who played a part in our rescue.

Ag and I learned that we're all part of one another. When the crunch comes, it doesn't really matter whether you're married or widowed, or single, or parents of one child or of ten. We're all part of the human family and are deeply responsible for one another. And so we're never really alone.

Today, our fellow passengers are scattered to their homes and their loved ones, all over the world, but Ag and I will always be linked to them by that experience of mutual suffering and caring and faith.

I learned something else, too. When those twenty-foot waves were threatening to swamp us, I knew that the assurance God had given me at Louis' bedside was real. I wasn't afraid to die. Not then, not ever.

THE FEARFUL SKIES

by Jimmy Stewart

Where does a man go to find courage?

The hour was late as I sat alone in a blacked-out Nissen hut, afraid of what the dawn would bring. It was a dark night in England during World War II, and I was flying B–24s (Liberators, the big four-engined bombers were called) as a squadron commander.

Our group had suffered heavy casualties during the day. As the big ships settled in for landing, wings and fuselages bore ragged holes from fighter attack and anti-aircraft fire. Bright red flares soared from planes carrying wounded, and ambulances raced to meet them. Men on the ground anxiously counted our own squadron's incoming planes ... nine ... ten ... eleven ... and then, only an empty grey sky. Where was the twelfth? Worried eyes swept the misty horizon, straining for some tiny dot, as hearts hoped against hope. But crew members in the returning planes knew that the missing ship would never land here again; German fighters had shot it down in flames.

Now there would be the painfully written letters to mothers, fathers and wives, along with prayers that some of the crew might have parachuted safely.

I stepped over to the little iron stove, scooped coal into it, and stared into the dull red embers. Tomorrow at dawn I would lead the squadron out again. Our target lay deep in enemy territory. Friendly fighters could accompany us only partway because of the distance involved. For much of the long flight we would be on our own – slow-moving targets for the German fighters, the barrel-chested FW–190s, the sleek ME–109s.

Imagination can be a serviceman's worst enemy. My forehead perspired as I visualised what would happen: My Liberator shuddering and lurching as we plowed through curtains of flak, the sky filled with the ugly brown-black shell-bursts, German fighters boring in from every direction.

I slumped down at my desk. Fear is an insidious and deadly thing. It can warp judgement, freeze reflexes, breed mistakes. Worse, it's contagious. I knew my own fear, if not checked, could infect my crew members. And I could feel it growing within me.

Out in the night, in some distant hangar, an aircraft engine growled into an increasing roar, then subsided into quiet as a night maintenance crew tested it for the upcoming mission.

I turned off the desk lamp, and my chair scraped the cement floor as I pushed it back. Walking to the window, I pulled back the blackout curtains and stared into the misty English night. My thoughts raced ahead to morning, all the things I had to do, all the plans I must remember for any emergency. How could I have a clear mind if it were saturated with fear?

What was the worst thing that could possibly happen? I asked myself. A flak-hit in the bomb bay? A fire in one of the wing tanks? A feathered propeller on a damaged engine that would bring the enemy fighters swooping in (they always singled out a crippled bomber)? One by one I hauled my worst fears out of the closet, as it were, and tried to face up to them. Was that the best way to conquer them? I wasn't sure.

Closing the curtains, I returned to my desk, snapped on the light, and pulled out a notebook. I began writing out a list of emergencies and how I would handle them. Everything I could think of. If our ship is mortally hit, I will try to get the crew out before I bail out – provided it doesn't blow up first. If I'm shot down and captured, I will reveal nothing but my name, rank and serial number. On and on, all the grim possibilities.

Finally, I finished writing and walked over to my metal cot. The springs creaked protestingly as I sat down. I stared unseeingly across the room. The deep-rooted fear was still there. It wouldn't go away.

I thought of my grandfather, who had fought in the Civil War, and my father, who had served in both the Spanish-American War and in the First World War. 'Were you afraid?' I'd asked as a youngster when we talked about Dad's experiences in France.

I could remember the faraway look in his eyes as he nodded. 'Every man is, son,' he said softly. 'Every man is.' But then he would always add something else. 'Just remember that you can't handle fear all by yourself, son. Give it to God: He'll carry it for you.'

My eyes misted as I remembered the letter Dad had given me when I left for England. He had written it at his old oak desk in his hardware store. I carried the worn and creased piece of paper always, and each time I read it, I seemed to learn something new:

'My dear Jim, soon after you read this letter you will be on your way to the worst sort of danger. I have had this in mind for a long time, and I am very concerned. But, Jim, I'm enclosing a copy of the ninety-first Psalm. The one thing that drives out fear and worry is the promise in it.

'I'm staking my faith in these words. I feel sure that God will lead you through this mad experience. I can say no more; I only continue to pray. God bless you and keep you. I love you more than I can tell you. Dad.'

I always choked up when I read that letter. Never before had Dad said that he loved me. I knew he did, but he had never said it. Until the letter.

Again, I read the psalm:

'Whoever goes to the Lord for safety … remains under the protection of the Almighty…. You need not fear any dangers at night or sudden attacks during the day … God will put His angels in charge of you to protect you wherever you go … they will hold you up with their hands.' What a promise for an airman!

There on the creaking cot with the night pressing in, I read those comforting words as a prayer. Then I relinquished to the Lord my fears for the coming day. I placed in His hands the squadron I would be leading. And, as the psalmist promised, I felt myself held up ...

Somewhere on a distant farm a cock crowed; dawn would be early. I got up and once more drew back the blackout curtains. The mist had cleared, and above the dark trees the sky was sparkling with stars.

I had no illusions about the mission that was coming up. I knew very well what might happen. And I knew that fear would ride with me. But I would live with it – and almost welcome it. Because, in its proper place, it would be an asset, sharpening perceptions, amplifying skills and heightening the capacity for quick decisions.

I had done all I could. I had faced each fear and handed it over. And now, no matter what might happen, I knew that God would be with me. In this world or the next.

A GLIMPSE OF PARADISE

by Josephine Crisler

A brush with death brings new meaning to life.

Many of us know some individual whose life has been revitalised by a brush with death. We know others whose concept of life eternal gives them an inner radiance. Call it what we will – a miracle, a vision, or a revelation – such experiences set up a chain reaction of inspiration to others.

I have had more than one such friend, and several of them were very young. There was a nineteen-year-old pilot, killed early in World War II. He had scribbled a poem on the back of an envelope and tucked it in his last letter home; it reached his family the day after news of his death. There are those who will tell you that it ranks with Keats and Shelley. Perhaps you have read John Magee's 'High Flight' which ends with that majestic line: 'I put out my hand and touched the face of God.'

The young poet's mother told me, 'I don't allow myself to think of the crash. I think instead of what he would want me to remember.'

But no amount of self-discipline can completely eradicate the very natural wonder as to what passed through the mind of a loved one when death approached. For these, there is comfort in the words of an eminent doctor, who told me: 'I have practised medicine for forty years. I have seen sudden death, and I have watched lingering death. Few people show any fear at the moment of passing, some, indeed, seem transfigured. My young brother was like that. At seventeen, he lay dying of a long and incurable illness. I was sitting beside him, my hand on his pulse, waiting for the end. He seemed too weak ever to move again.

'Suddenly, he sat bolt upright, crying: "Oh, isn't that beautiful? Isn't that the most glorious music you ever heard?"

'His face was radiant as he fell back in my arms, dead. I, who would have rejected the speculative proof of a theologian, could not reject the fact that my young brother, in the moment of his passing, had seen and heard something incredibly beautiful, something I could neither see nor hear.'

But most spectacular of all is the experience of Mrs Counts, who met death, and who no longer fears it, because – as she told me – 'while I was "away", I had a glimpse of Paradise.' Lest you should think she is some sort of crank, let me assure you that she is one of the sanest, most intelligent and consistently hardworking individuals of my acquaintance. She supports herself and her mother in the highly competitive business of estate agency. Here is her story as she told it to me:

'We were returning from a visit to our married daughter. A man driving a truck pulled out of line on a hill ... he had been drinking ... the black-top road was wet. When he saw us, he slammed on his brakes. I have no memory of the crash. My glasses were imbedded in my face ... my jaw was broken in five places.' Her voice dropped a little. 'I am so grateful. I could have been blinded or terribly mutilated.

'My first moment of consciousness was the realisation that I had "come back" from something so beautiful, I can't describe it even to myself. Every night before I go to sleep, I try to recapture it again. I remember trees and flowers, colour and the most glorious light!' Her voice trembled and for a moment I thought she would not go on. Then she said, 'The beauty of it was secondary, really ... It was the utter peace ... the sense of security ... the sure conviction that everything was all right. You see, I had been a chronic worrier all my life ... about bills, about every little problem ... about things that never even happened.

'But during those seven months, when I had to be fed through a tube, I never seemed to mind the pain. I felt only gratitude for the revelation of divine love that had come to me.'

At this point I interrupted: 'Now that you seem to have lost all fear of death, do you want to die?'

'Lots of people have asked me that. I can only tell you that I love life and I want to live as long as I can be useful. As a matter of fact,' she added, 'life is ever so much better in every way. I have quit worrying and fretting. If there is something I can do about a situation, I do it. If not, I put that problem behind me and go on to something I can do something about.

'I shrink from trying to force my own thoughts on people who have a different viewpoint, but if I knew that death would come tomorrow, or next week, it would seem as natural as a journey. I wish all those who are afraid and those who mourn, could know what I know, that I had a glimpse of Paradise. There is indeed no death; what seems so is transition.'

3

WHEN HOPE
IS RESTORED

*Hope is the dove flying across the watery wastes
with a leafy twig in its beak. When things
are dark it's amazing the way God rekindles
the spark of hope in our hearts with
what can be quite tiny moments of joy.*

Wendy Craig

THE POSTCARD

by Chris Spencer

What chance was there that it would ever be received?

In war-torn Beirut, Lebanon, in January 1987, Church of England envoy Terry Waite was kidnapped by the extremist group Hezbullah. People around the world began to pray for his safety and release.

In the town of Bedford, fifty miles north of London, a British housewife, Joy Brodier, joined in the prayers for Terry that were included in the regular service of her Baptist church. But Joy did something more. She put her prayers on paper.

One day after the second anniversary of Terry's capture, Joy happened upon a postcard depicting a memorable event in her town's history. In the seventeenth century, the preacher John Bunyan was imprisoned in a Bedford jail for his religious beliefs, and during his long imprisonment he wrote the classic *Pilgrim's Progress*. The picture on Joy's postcard was of a stained-glass window showing John Bunyan in his cell.

Struck by the similar circumstances of the two men, Joy picked up the postcard and on the back of it penned a message for Terry: 'People everywhere are praying for you and working for your release and the release of the other hostages.' She signed it, and then hesitated. How to address it? Finally she wrote all she knew, all anyone knew: Terry Waite, c/o Hezbullah (Party of God), Beirut, Lebanon.

The card sat for a day on Joy's mantelpiece next to her clock. Her husband, Graham, glanced at it and said incredulously, 'You're going to send this?' Joy shrugged and nodded.

At the post office she handed the postcard to the clerk and asked, 'How much?' The clerk looked at it, scratched her head and then matter-of-factly charged Joy the normal rate for an airmail postcard to Beirut.

Three years passed. Three years of rumours, bulletins, war, stalled negotiations and continued prayers for the release of the hostages. Then in 1991 word came that Terry Waite and US hostage Tom Sutherland were being freed.

At last, on 19 November, Terry Waite landed on British soil. In an airport hangar he spoke to the waiting journalists and TV cameras. At noon that same day in Bedford, Joy Brodier watched the news on television. She heard a haggard but jubilant Terry speak of his 1,763 days in prison, his hope for the release of the other prisoners and his gratitude to all the people who had been praying for him. In particular he mentioned a postcard, the only piece of mail that had reached him in nearly five years.

He described it: 'A picture of a stained-glass window from Bedford showing John Bunyan in jail.'

It can't be, Joy thought. 'It has to be,' her husband said. Four weeks later a letter arrived from Terry Waite. 'It's my turn to write to you,' he began.

How Joy's postcard got to him was nothing short of amazing. Even the guard who delivered it to Terry was amazed. For five years Terry's whereabouts had been a secret. The International Red Cross couldn't reach him. The British Embassy in Beirut had boxes full of cards and letters that they couldn't deliver. And yet Joy's postcard reached him.

Then one summer Joy Brodier and Terry Waite finally met in person. Standing beneath the stained-glass window at the Bunyan Meeting House in Bedford, Terry thanked Joy for what he described as the 'simple act' that gave him such hope in his own captivity.

A simple act, indeed, and though the odds against her postcard getting through were staggering, Joy Brodier proved what power there can be in a tiny deed done in great faith.

A STRANGE PLACE TO HOPE

by Corrie ten Boom

A Dutch heroine tells the gripping personal story of victory over despair and humiliation.

Rank upon rank we stood that hot September morning in 1944, more than a thousand women lining the railroad siding, one unspoken thought among us: Not Germany!

Beside me my sister Betsie swayed. I was fifty-two, Betsie fifty-nine. These eight months in a concentration camp since we had been caught concealing Jews in our home had been harder on her. But prisoners though we were, at least till now we had remained in Holland. And now when liberation must come any day, where were they taking us?

Behind us guards were shouting, prodding us with their guns. Instinctively my hand went to the string around my neck. From it, hanging down my back between my shoulder blades, was the small cloth bag that held our Bible, that forbidden book which had not only sustained Betsie and me throughout these months, but given us strength to share with our fellow prisoners. So far we had kept it hidden. But if we should go to Germany – we had heard tales of the prison inspections there.

A long line of empty boxcars was rolling slowly past. Now it clanged to a halt and a gaping freight door loomed in front of us. I helped Betsie over the steep side. The dark boxcar grew quickly crowded. We were pressed against the sides. It was a small European freight car, with thirty or forty people jammed in it. And still the guards drove women in, pushing, jabbing with their guns. It was only when eighty women were packed inside that the heavy door slid shut and we heard the iron bolts driven into place outside.

Women were sobbing and many fainted although in the tight-wedged crowd they remained upright. The sun beat down on the motionless train, the temperature in the packed car rose. It was hours before the packed train gave a sudden lurch and began to move. Almost at once it stopped again, then again crawled forward. The rest of that day and all night long it was the same, stopping, starting, slamming, jerking. Once through a slit in the side of the car I saw trainmen carrying a length of twisted rail. Maybe the tracks ahead were destroyed. Maybe we would still be in Holland when liberation came. But at dawn we rolled through the Dutch border town of Emmerich. We were in Germany.

For two more incredible days and two more nights we were carried deeper and deeper into the land of our fears.

Worse than the crush of bodies and the filth was the thirst. Two or three times when the train was stopped the door was slid open a few inches and a pail of water passed in. But we had become animals, incapable of planning, those nearest the door got it all.

At last, on the morning of the fourth day, the door was hauled open its full width. Only a handful of very young soldiers was there to order us out and march us off. No more were needed. We could scarcely walk, let alone resist. From the crest of a small hill we saw it, the end of our journey, a vast grey barracks city surrounded by double concrete walls.

'Ravensbrück!'

Like a whispered curse, the word passed back through the line. This was the notorious women's death camp itself, the very symbol to Dutch hearts of all that was evil.

As we stumbled down the hill, I felt the Bible bumping on my back. As long as we had that, I thought, we could face even hell itself. But how could we conceal it through the inspection I knew lay ahead? It was the middle of the night when Betsie and I reached the processing barracks. And there under the harsh ceiling lights we saw a dismaying sight. As each woman reached the head of the line she had to strip off every scrap of clothes, throw them all onto a pile guarded by soldiers, and walk naked past the scrutiny of a dozen guards into the shower room. Coming out of the shower room, she wore only the thin regulation prison dress and a pair of shoes.

Our Bible! How could we take it past so many watchful eyes?

'Oh, Betsie!' I began – and then stopped at the sight of her pain-whitened face. As a guard strode by I begged him in German to show us the toilets. He jerked his head in the direction of the shower room. 'Use the drain holes!' he snapped. Timidly Betsie and I stepped out of line and walked forward to the huge room with its row on row of overhead spigots. It was empty, waiting for the next batch of fifty naked and shivering women.

A few minutes later we would return here stripped of everything we possessed. And then we saw them, stacked in a corner, a pile of old wooden benches crawling with cockroaches, but to us the furniture of heaven itself. In an instant I had slipped the little bag over my head and stuffed it behind the benches.

And so it was that when we were herded into that room ten minutes later, we were not poor, but rich. Rich in the care of Him who was God even of Ravensbrück.

Of course when I put on the flimsy prison dress, the Bible bulged beneath it. But that was His business, not mine. At the exit, guards were feeling every prisoner, front, back and sides. The woman ahead of me was searched. Behind me, Betsie was searched. They did not touch or even look at me.

Outside the building was a second ordeal, another line of guards examining each prisoner again. I slowed down as I reached them, but the captain shoved me roughly by the shoulder. 'Move along! You're holding up the line!'

So Betsie and I came to our barracks at Ravensbrück. Before long we were holding clandestine Bible study groups for an ever-growing group, and Barracks 28 became known throughout the camp as 'the crazy place, where they hope'.

Yes, hoped, in spite of all that human madness could do. We had learned that a stronger power had the final word, even here.

WHEN LOVE FAILS

by Hannah Pierson

A story of childhood despair that brought great courage.

My sister, Katie, and I are trapped in the kitchen with our mother. She is giving us shots of blood-red vinegar. Even if I swallow quickly, the sharply acidic taste remains in my mouth. She holds my face toward her as her thumb pushes in under my jawbone. I used to admire the crystal shot glasses kept in Gran's cabinet, but now the glass is thick and cold as my mother forces the caustic punishment down my throat.

It is a few years later. I am eight. I am sitting at the dining room table with *Strong's Exhaustive Concordance of the Bible*. It is an immense book with tiny type. There are no sentences, only phrases, abbreviations and reference numbers. I love to read; I have a list of the books I have read this year, but *Strong's* does not have stories in it. The leather-bound King James Bible has stories in it, but my task is to find all of the verses under the bold heading that read 'tale-bearer'; after that, 'liar'. Then I write out the relevant Bible passages in their entirety. My only recourse is to do as I am told, so that maybe this will not happen again. It starts to get dark. My fingers hurt and I get thirsty, but I stay at the table until I am all done.

I accept these 'disciplinary measures'. They are not painful like the under-the-chin punches that do not leave much of a visible mark. As I get older the injustice strikes me harder. Words cause me the most pain. The words last much longer than the bruises. My mother wishes out loud that I had never been born. She destroys my self-confidence. I have developed a sort of cynicism – I doubt that people could honestly be good to me, that they could like me.

I have no sense of security or trust. I find a kitchen knife on the floor in my room and wonder what was contemplated while I slept. Sometimes I try to hide, alone and scared, in a dark, cold cellar or garage. Sometimes we fight all night. I struggle to get away until she becomes bored or tired. It is futile for a child to try to escape from the bathroom when a large and strong woman blocks the door. Grandpa threatens to call the police, but he never does. He is afraid of her too. My head aches. Welts rise on my arms. Blood rushes to my face as I feel my cheek grow warm under her hand-print. Her anger comes from something other than my failings. Something else sets her off, but she attacks Katie, Gran and me. I am the strongest, the angriest, and I fight back. I do things to distract her from them, like throw her diet lemonade on her worn blue bathrobe; then her hatred is turned to me. But I am only a weak child, and I cannot do anything to make it all stop.

Sometimes my mother speaks with no emotion, no expression on her face. It scares me when she is hollow like this, because I know she is agitated, perhaps on the verge of an explosive wrath. I do not want to upset her. I am afraid of messing up. I am always treading on thin ice. My efforts to avoid confrontation by careful obedience are doomed to fail. I have become a meticulous perfectionist, a neat child to those who do not know. People think I have good manners. I am unheard and unseen; I just watch. I have plenty of time to study my family members because I am observant and am sensitive to what the people in my house are feeling and thinking. It is like keeping track of the pieces on a chessboard. It is necessary that I know how each piece moves and how the opponent will react. I do not worry about winning, just keeping myself out of check.

I start sixth grade at a new school. Katie goes too. I try not to be noticed. This is difficult because my class is small and other kids are nice to me. I go to their birthday parties and eat dinner at their houses; maybe they like me a little. Their mums seem nice, but my mum can seem nice too. My teacher is more than just nice; she understands. Mrs Hoffman must remember what it was like to be a kid.

I work hard in school. If I do really well, my mum might not get so angry with me. Dad might notice that I exist. He might listen. He might be around more. He spends plenty of time with other kids; he directs the youth group at church. I bring home almost perfect report cards, but he does not say 'Good job'. I work hard anyway because I am learning. I am learning that there is much more that I want to know.

Dad comes home late at night, wearing his leather jacket, after youth group. He smells like bowling alleys and pizza. He sits on the edge of the bed. Dad says that Mum might have to go away for a while to get some help. Instead of this sudden information solving my problems, it adds to them. Information preceded by 'Don't let your mother know' is dangerous. If my collusion is discovered later, the consequences will be severe. Katie is worried, and I try to comfort her.

Mrs Hoffman can tell that I haven't slept. She does not know that my mother had her hands around my throat last night. I talk to her. I tell her some of what is going on. She goes with me to the headmaster. I cry because I know it may only get worse from here. They give me dry, papery Kleenex. When my dad picks Katie and me up from school, we cannot go home. Katie cries, she does not want to leave Mum. My dad says he is taking us away. We end up at a foster home in the next state. It is a Christian family, and they pray for us. The family already has plenty of kids. Eventually, Dad, Katie and I move back together without Mum.

The next years are filled with lawyers and social workers. A psychiatrist evaluates us. He says my sister and I are okay. I think Katie and I have learned to cope with a lot. I have to go to court. One of my teachers gives me an index card with verses on it to give me courage. These are kind verses from the Bible, not a punishment or condemnation. They are not about tale-bearers. God says He will be there even when your father and mother forsake you.

I have not had a mother in an emotional sense; now I do not even have one physically present. I am the oldest. I am independent and responsible; I have to be. Some of my friends have Mums who wrap sandwiches in cling-film for packed lunches. Their mothers do their laundry for them, come to their school meetings, and make sure their dresses fit. I buy the fabric for my dress with my own money, and I sew it myself.

I still have my dad, but he cannot fill the void where two parents should be. He is still the same. A woman who is also a youth group leader is my father's wife now.

My mother still haunts my daily existence. She calls at my school, my house, my friends' mothers. She shows up at my church. She follows me and makes threats. She tells people that I am a terrible person. She throws the tea that they serve after church onto our car. Restraining orders are only pieces of paper. When she is committed to a hospital, it just makes her more angry. Gran insists she is sick, that I should not hold it against her. Christ commanded us to love everyone. I go to visit my mother. She is with the insane people on the tenth floor. I appease Gran. I should forgive. Later, I think I do.

It is difficult for me to love. I have started with accepting myself. Even though my mum wished I had not been born, I could not be happier to be alive. I have found that there are people who really do love me for who I am. To really love, I have to trust first. My trust is hard to earn because I have lost a lot by trusting a little. Maybe I am not emotional because I do not find love quickly, but I am emotional in the sense that I value love more because I perceive it as rare. God's love is abundant, yet rare in its perfection. I have been looking for faithfulness and unconditional love among my fellow imperfect human beings. Now as I face questions about my future, I can look back and see how God has carried me through. He has been faithful. As I fall away, He calls me back. Sometimes I think I have to study, to search for God or receive a sign. When I stop searching and just think about all that He has done for me, faith, trust and love become so simple.

A SYMBOL OF HOPE

by Marjorie Holmes

When God speaks in whispers.

My mother always savoured sunsets until the last lingering glow had faded from the sky.

'Just look at that sunset now!' Mother was always urging us. 'You can peel those potatoes later. Your homework can wait.' We must stop whatever we were doing to follow her pleased gaze. 'Isn't that the most beautiful sky you've ever seen?'

Then, after supper when the bright hues had melted into the dusk and there was nothing left of the sunset but a last stubborn band of burning rose, she would return to the porch a minute and stand there, arms wrapped in her apron against the chill, and murmur: 'The afterglow means hope.'

What could hope possibly mean to this middle-aged married woman whose dreams must surely all be behind her?

I was puzzled. I sensed her hopes but dimly: that the problems of her family would be resolved, wounds healed, frictions cease, worries vanish … the doctor's report would be favourable … my brother wouldn't have to have an operation, after all that new company would be offering work soon, and Dad would land a better job … there would at last be enough money to go around … her children's turbulent lives would get straightened out – the boys would find themselves, the girls would marry the right sweethearts.

Hope? What did it mean to her? It spoke of that marvellous ingredient that keeps humanity going – something that is almost as

132

vital to people as love – God-given hope, belief in tomorrow, bright expectations that refuse to die.

It was surely what Jesus himself was talking about when He counselled His followers to be of good cheer, not to despair; when He said that we should not only have life, but have it more abundantly.

My mother gave her children the gift of sunsets. But an even greater gift was her gift of the afterglow: the message she read in those remaining embers, burning like little fires of faith long after the sunset itself was gone, a lighted bridge across the coming darkness to the stars, 'The afterglow means hope.'

BREAKTHROUGH IN BELFAST

by Monica Patterson

An unusual group of women bring new hope for peace in a city dark with hate and violence.

As the sky glowed red over Belfast that night from fires raging through blocks of homes, I could only cry helplessly for those who suffered. I was not yet aware of the intensity with which these fires would burn into my life.

In 1966, when my husband's work brought us to Belfast from England, the hate which set fires like these had not yet developed. But now, in 1970, it was raging.

It swirled across cobblestone streets through which armoured trucks growled. It exploded in bombs, cracked in sniper bullets, screamed in men dragged off to internment camps.

From history I knew this hate was spawned in an ancient conflict of two Northern Ireland peoples, the Celtic Catholic minority who felt discrimination by the Protestant English-settler descendants, who in turn feared a growing Catholic civil rights movement.

I saw both sides wave their religious labels like military banners, and no man, woman or child seemed untouched by the hate. Behind barred doors families huddled before TV screens which spewed venom nightly through endless debates and counter-charges.

In Ireland, housewives and mothers like myself are expected to remain in the background. But the senseless violence anguished me. It particularly stabbed me one evening when I picked up our newspaper and saw a photo of tykes hurling rocks and bottles. It was captioned: 'The Men and Women of Tomorrow'.

My heart cried out for an answer. It came when a friend who knew my concern suggested, 'Monica, go have a talk with Ruth Agnew.'

Earlier my friend had written a letter to the newspaper pleading for peace. He had signed it, which was unusual. In Belfast few letters to the editor are ever signed; no one wants to step out of line. Because of his letter, Ruth Agnew had contacted my friend.

I found Ruth living in a little kitchen house, a type of row house common in Belfast. A widow in her late fifties, she had been a cleaner in a gas plant for thirty years. As we sat over tea, she said falteringly, 'I've had a conviction that the women could do something.'

I left Ruth's house with conflicting emotions. I was never a joiner. Moreover, I was in a peculiar position in a society bedevilled by the word 'loyalty', where one is expected to identify with this side or that and then pay it unquestioning allegiance. For I was a Roman Catholic from England.

But as a crowd of schoolchildren shrieked past waving wooden guns, I knew that I, too, must step out of line.

Belfast has long been divided into polarised areas, such as Shankill Road, where Protestants live, and The Falls, a Catholic settlement.

I began to follow up leads in those areas, talking with women's groups and individual women. I heard a lot about social justice. I knew that was important, but something spoke to me which said: 'No, we want something from far deeper in the human spirit, something that steps beyond the boundaries of political debate.'

And then it occurred to me. We would have to bring women of both sides together to work for peace. But many of our church leaders had told us this was not possible. The situation was too delicate.

But some of us, I felt, were going to have to be fools for the sake of peace. It would not be enough simply to pray for peace and then pass by on the other side. We must involve ourselves actively with the same dedication as those who believe in violence.

After six weeks' search I found fifteen Catholic and Protestant women willing to try. One afternoon we sat down together around a table in a large house in Belfast. We agreed that we rejected violence as a means of attaining any goal. Then another problem arose. We had decided to invite all Belfast women to a meeting to explain our goal. But it was difficult to find a large hall in a bomb-free area. Finally I found one.

We ran an advert in the Belfast papers inviting 'women opposed to violence who wish to dedicate themselves to peace'. Buses would bring them to the hall.

Wednesday evening found us at the hall nervously checking details. The meeting was to start at 8.00. As the big hall clock struck eight, we edged onto the stage. I looked into the seats and my heart froze. Only six people sat there. I was panic stricken.

Suddenly the auditorium doors flew open and in surged the women, hundreds of them, ordinary working-class women from Protestant Shankill Road, from the Catholic Falls, from many areas. The buses had been tied up in traffic.

At 8.15 we prayed together, then had a cup of tea and presented our programme for peace. But there was a coolness in that auditorium as the meeting wore on. I could sense the mutual suspicion.

Suddenly a woman from The Falls stood up, her grey sweater hanging loosely. The room hushed as every eye fastened on her.

She stood quietly for a moment, then extended her arms and in a tremulous voice pleaded: 'I want to shake hands with a woman from the Shankill.'

An explosion of warmth flooded the room as if something long confined to the depths had broken through the surface. In an instant Protestant women from Shankill and Catholic women from The Falls arose and, with hands extended, moved towards each other.

That night was the real beginning of Women Together. The movement has grown to a thousand Catholic and Protestant women who meet regularly in small mixed groups to work for peace in their own neighbourhoods. All that they do is in the spirit of love which they have found to be stronger than hate.

Love joined the small group of Protestant and Catholic women who stood arm in arm fending off opposing bands of fighters. Love gives courage to those who go to the aid of the victims of the bombing despite threats, who open their homes to refugees of another religion from strife-torn areas. And a new light dawns in the eyes of a child who sees his mother standing arm in arm with the 'enemy'.

Fuelled by implicit trust in each other, they become super-women. One woman stopped a riot starting in a factory; two women encouraged 200 would-be rioters to go to church to pray for peace.

Their work is not without payment. Pelted with eggs and toma-toes, derided by some reporters as the Petticoat Brigade, the women have received threatening phone calls, abuse in the street, even intimidation from relatives.

Yet, respect for them grows. Whenever a boy or man was held by the British army for questioning, if a local Women Together member could vouch for his innocence, the captive was released.

This is because the women are known for not taking sides. Instead, they walk down the middle of the road so they can extend their arms both ways in love.

In one respect that policy raises a problem in financing our activities. Because of our non-partisanship, we shy away from government money, as it would make us suspect by those of the other side. And so we depend on individual contributions.

Today there are more than a dozen local Women Together groups, and the number grows.

We also gain strength through the WT Minute. Each evening at 6.45, we stop for a minute to pray that we may be instruments for peace, and to mourn the suffering.

Beyond emergency aid, Women Together take Protestant and Catholic children on picnics together, open playgrounds and youth clubs, take meals to the elderly and sponsor mixed groups on holidays. On one such trip some Protestant extremists found themselves staying in a convent and were surprised at 'how nice those nuns treated us'. We are now expanding into all of Northern Ireland. Hopefully, we will become that bridge through which both sides will learn to live with each other again in love and understanding.

Concerned with those men and women of tomorrow, we are now planning Children Together. Will there be a Husbands Together? In a sense there already is, for now many of us couldn't carry on without the moral and practical support of our husbands.

Women Together proudly witnesses their stand by wearing a button with a picture of a dove. Originally this dove simply stood as a symbol of peace. However, as I think back on the mysterious ways in which we have been guided, of the insurmountable problems overcome, of the miracles that have been wrought, I realise from whom our help has come.

Morning Prayer

Give me the strength to meet each day
With quiet will.
Give me the faith to know you are
My Shepherd still.
Give me the light to find my way
When shadows fall.
Be my steady, guiding star,
Father of all.

Hebrew Union Home Prayer Book

THE LAST LEAF

by Anita Wade

Hope hangs on.

I noticed it one November morning, away at college and fighting some perplexing personal battles. The tree outside our window stood stark and bare, its leaves, shrivelled and dead, had fallen to the waiting earth. Except for one. Pale, taut, sapped of its nourishing juices, it clung tenaciously to the very top of the tree.

One leaf left. One leaf alone against the wind and chilling snow flurries, hanging on for its life, refusing to give in to nature's persistent invitation to die.

There was something poetic about the way that leaf resisted as long as it did, high at the top, long after the others had gone the way of millions of leaves before them. Day after day, as we watched the little drama through our kitchen window, some of my room-mates openly cheered the leaf's courage. 'Hang in there,' they'd say. A few shrugged. 'What's the matter with you? It's just a stupid leaf.'

Then one quiet moment, as I stood by the window alone, I gleaned an invaluable lesson from that pathetic little leaf.

Illuminated by lights from nearby apartments, it still clung stubbornly to the top of the naked tree, and watching it, I was suddenly filled with hope – warming, uplifting, healing hope. It was as if God were telling me that when everything grimly crumbles, when the crowd drifts away without me, when the very elements seem to oppose and torment, I can turn to Him for hope and strength to cling to the top and refuse to be defeated.

The next morning the leaf had finally fallen and been blown away. I knew it eventually would, of course. And like many last hopes, perhaps it was crushed by a careless passer-by.

But there would be more in the Spring, I thought. There is always hope.

SUNDAY AT SEA

by Douglas Wardrop

An unforgettable adventure story.

I suppose we all have fears of the unknown, few of which ever come to pass. Yet on Sunday morning, 9 June 1957, one fear that had haunted me actually happened.

I was second mate on the *British Monarch,* a freighter, and we were in the Pacific, hundreds of miles from land, en route to Japan.

It was 4 a.m. I went to the stern to inspect a faulty log clock. Unable to read the clock standing on the deck, I climbed on top of a bulwark. While leaning outboard, the ship lurched slightly and I lost my balance. A desperate grab at the bulwark missed.

I fell into the ocean.

When I came gasping to the surface, the *Monarch*'s stern lights were disappearing into the darkness. I shouted but no one heard me.

I had the feeling that I wanted to shake myself hard and wake up in my bunk. Certainly this was the bad dream I'd had so many times of falling overboard at night and finding myself all alone in the vast ocean. But this was no dream. This was my worst nightmare come true.

The awful truth of my situation struck home. My ship was now out of sight; it might be hours before they discovered my disappearance.

Panicky thoughts came. I had a million-to-one chance of survival. Should I end it quickly? Just let myself go under?

Suddenly I desperately wanted to live. At twenty-three, life seemed very sweet and desirable.

I tried floating on my back, but the waves kept washing over my face and filling my nose with water. The easiest way to stay afloat, I soon discovered, was to tread water, with my feet and arms describing an arc in front of my body.

It took surprisingly little effort to keep afloat. Must be a lot of salt in the water – why, I can last for hours! If only I weren't so alone.

And then it came to me, 'I'm not alone. No one ever really is. For God is with me all the time, unseen, unheard, but very real.' And the first pangs of panic subsided.

Should I get rid of my clothing? It was light tropical stuff and didn't weigh me down much. Then, too, it might give protection against fish. I decided to keep on all my clothes, including shoes. Shoes, particularly, might help if sharks came.

Right then I realised my thoughts could take two directions: they could dwell on the potential horrors of the situation or they could fix on the possibilities of survival.

'Poor Captain Coutts,' I thought out loud. 'I'd hate to be in your shoes now, debating what to do. Can you find a dot in the ocean, Captain?'

A sharp needle-like pain shot through my left leg. An electric eel moved away and began to circle around me. He was about two feet long with small, pale blue suckers.

The eel continued to circle, ugly and sinister in the murky water. 'God, I've been told that everything you make in this world has a purpose, but surely not a mean and vicious one.' After a while the eel disappeared.

It got hot. Hours passed. I began to ramble a bit to myself and a bit to God. 'Well, God, I'm in your hands,' I said aloud. 'In you I put my trust for better or worse. But if you don't mind my inject-ing an idea of my own, I just don't believe my time is up.'

Then a turtle appeared. He was enormous. 'Hi there, Turty!' I called. The turtle inspected me for a while with blinking eyes, then decided that I was harmless.

'Turty, how did you get so fat way out here?' I asked. The turtle looked at me so solemnly that I actually laughed. A real laugh. Was I losing my mind?

More hours passed. Now the beginning of weakness. I tried floating on my back again. A wave passed over my face. I gulped, coughed and sputtered. That wouldn't do: too much loss of strength.

If the *Monarch* were coming back, shouldn't she be here by now? Or had she already gone by me?

Once I saw what looked like an enormous fish coming my way. Sharks! I was surprised they hadn't come before. But I was too weak to do anything but stare. But it wasn't a shark. I shook the water out of my blurry eyes.

A little later I saw two masts on the horizon. I tried to wave my arms, but they weighed a ton each. 'Please, God, don't let them come so close and not see me. I'm not afraid to die, but don't add torment.'

And then they were lowering a boat. The *Monarch* had returned!

Later Captain Coutts was shaking his head in amazement. 'I can hardly believe it. I told myself over and over that it was a waste of time to turn around, but something refused to let me give up.'

I was in the water nine hours. The *Monarch* covered a hundred miles before she found me. My shipmates kidded me later. 'Our money's on you in the next channel race,' said one. Another chimed in, 'What a way to spend Sunday at sea.'

Sunday at sea! I liked that phrase. For isn't Sunday the day you're supposed to feel closest to your Creator?

REASON FOR HOPE

by Jaime Blissford

An explorer discovers something unique.

Mungo Park, the explorer, one day was stranded alone in an African wilderness. Nearly dead from hunger, thirst and exhaustion, he decided there was no hope for survival and stretched out on the ground to await death.

But then a small flower of exceptional beauty caught his eye. He said, 'Though the whole plant was no larger than one of my fingers, I could not contemplate the delicate conformation of its roots, leaves, and capsules without admiration.

'Can the Being who planted, watered, and brought to perfection, in this obscure part of the world, a thing which appears of so small importance, look with unconcern upon the situation and suffering of creatures formed after His own image? Surely not.' He started out again and, disregarding both hunger and fatigue, travelled forward until he reached safety.

PIECES AND PATCHES

by Diane Robb

Sometimes, when sorrow rips the very fabric of life, mending begins with hope.

That September, when I discovered I was expecting a second child, I set out to sew a winter coat. I chose an expensive heather-coloured wool and a soft sapphire-blue lining, with warm insulating material between. The very idea made me feel warm, and settled, and secure. As the last crickets of summer clicked outside the window, I imagined myself ankle-deep in February fluff, cloaked in soft armour against the slanting sting of ice and snow.

But in mid-October I started to miscarry. I knew it was over as one whose reserves of hope have been depleted by long years of infertility can know. A quick dilatation and curettage proved the inevitable. No baby had formed.

After the jarring reality, the sad announcements and the quiet visitors, it proved to be not such a devastating loss. It was more a small pain that stunned. A few weeks later I found the courage to gather the shambles of the half-sewn coat and stuff them into a bag at the back of the closet for another time.

The strong instinct for nesting, caring and creating shifted focus once again to my two-year-old daughter. I began to make her a teddy, and at the last minute I remembered the insulating material I had bought for the coat. Why not use it? I certainly won't be needing it, I thought, surprised at the accompanying stab of bitterness.

The piece of material was only a yard wide, but it ran the length of the teddy. It covered all but a girl's outstretched limbs, as her father's warm hand had once covered her tiny new-born body.

In June I became pregnant again. A busy work schedule and a pessimism kept me from all but the most guarded sense of joy. In late August I miscarried again.

I couldn't grieve. I felt hard and cold, ruthless in my detachment from pain. I cleaned rooms, repainted the house. But this time I lacked the feeling of being able to pick up and move on. This time a door had closed. Without regret, or much feeling at all, I gave away all my maternity clothes.

Except for the half-finished coat. I avoided going into the sewing room. Yet the coat bag was always there, an unfinished chapter.

A fancy-dress party for my daughter approached. While searching the shops for material to line the inside of my daughter's costume, it occurred to me that I had a perfectly respectable candidate at home: the lining of the coat. Guiltily, I cut into the soft blue fabric to make the lining of her hood. But when I led a woolly-hatted Elephant Queen into the bright pools of porch light, it seemed precisely right. Later I borrowed the big zipper bought for the coat to use in another project.

The bag began to empty. And I was spending time in the sewing room again. I began to understand that I wasn't just making good use of materials from a project long abandoned; I was diffusing the anger and bitterness of broken dreams and transforming it into the substance of living. For the first time in months, I felt better.

I began taking stock of other areas of my life. I discovered a Pandora's box of psychological liabilities and diminished expectations that held a marvellous potential to be transformed into better things. I started the job of emotional housecleaning by taking a load of old clothes and children's things to a local charity. I cut up two high-school ski jackets of sentimental value to make my daughter a snowsuit. When the annual chore of removing the dead growth from the flower garden came around, I carefully tapped the dried seeds from the dead blooms, gathering the ingredients that would become next year's Spring.

None of these things were very remarkable. Some I had done before. But never in the spirit of deliberately taking something negative and extracting the very last ounce of good out of it.

Gradually I was able to apply my new perspective to more volatile personal issues. I came to see error and misfortune not as stumbling blocks but as influences, in the current of change. I stopped thinking of the possibility of having another child as the point around which all other considerations of happiness revolved.

It didn't always work. To believe that all bad things can be transformed into good is a philosophy destined to disillusion. But the debris of loss has its usefulness. It rebuilds and changes shape. It changes hope. And sometimes, sparkling among the ruins, treasures can be found: courage, resolve and self-acceptance.

Last Autumn I emptied the coat bag. I took the shapeless wool garment and cut it into long narrow strips, coiling them together in a soft wheel with other woollen fabrics to be braided into a rug. Whenever it's finished – in a few years, or a lifetime – I fully expect it to be spilled on, pulled back, bunched up and enjoyed. It may never have to suffer the soils of a new baby's dribbling grin, or a toddler's spilled apple juice. But then again, maybe it will.

OUT THERE SOMEWHERE

by Frank Richardson

A fading snapshot taken over forty years ago was all he knew of the mother who had vanished from his life.

For years Mother's Day was one of the most difficult times of the year for me. As a radio news-announcer, each May – as that is the month it is celebrated in the States – I would find myself relating stories and reminding listeners that it was once again time to honour our mothers. I had little enthusiasm for it, because I could never honour my own mother.

The reason was that I had never known my mother. I didn't even know what had happened to her. My father refused to speak of her. When I was a youngster I'd ask him about her and wonder why she had left me, but his mouth would form a tight line and he'd look away. All I was ever able to get from Dad was that he had been married briefly before going into the Navy during World War II, and I ended up being raised by his parents.

Later, when I was seventeen, my grandmother, after much prodding on my part, got out some snapshots taken in 1942. They showed me, a toddler, with my young mother, who'd been only sixteen when I was born. But when I asked the inevitable questions, Grandmother merely sighed and said, 'Oh, Frankie, I'm sure it was for the best.'

The best? I wondered. Whose best?

Even after I had grown up, joined the Army, and eventually returned and began my work in broadcasting, the questions continued to haunt me: Why had my mother left me? Where was she now? Did she long for me as I longed for her? Or was I the son of a mother who did not want me and had never loved me? When I worked at a radio station in Richmond, for a time I tried to dig up some information about my mother. But I had no success.

In 1977 I came to my present job as a morning news-announcer at a local radio station. I married, and my wife and I had a son, Joey. I thought I could see my mother in his dark brown eyes. Mine are brown too, and since most of the relatives I knew had blue eyes, I believed my mother's eyes had to be brown.

The years went by. After my grandparents died, my father was the only one left who knew anything about my mother. Despite my questions, he maintained his silence. Finally I gave up trying to break it.

Still, I would pray that I might meet my mother, feeling that she was out there somewhere. I would ask God to take care of her. And I would read my Bible, the one my grandmother had given to me when I was nine years old. Billy Graham and his team had signed it when I met them at age thirteen. The one verse that spoke to me was all about waiting and hoping. Was God telling me simply to wait? In the late summer of 1985, for some reason the urge to find my mother intensified. One morning I reported for work as usual and aired a news item about the crash of a jetliner. As I related the dramatic story of how a surviving stewardess, Vicki Chavis, had been found dangling from a seat in the rear of the L–1011, I couldn't get the thought of my mother out of my mind. I began to redouble my prayers about her.

Finally, late on an icy Friday night the following January, my father telephoned. 'Son,' he said, sounding a bit strained, 'I know you've been wondering about your mother for some time. I, uh … I, well, I've always thought it was something that belonged in the past. But, here's a number where you can reach her.' He gave me the number, then added in resignation, 'I'll leave it up to you, son.'

I hung up the phone, dumbfounded. What had caused him to change his mind? I looked down at the number I had scribbled. It was much too late to call. I'd do it in the morning.

But would I? Should I? After crawling into bed I couldn't sleep. Questions nagged me. Did my mother even want to hear from me? After all, as far as I knew, she had never made an attempt to get in touch with me during my forty-two years. Would my coming back into her life upset her?

And what kind of person would she be? Would I like her? Would I approve of her lifestyle? Would my longing for a loving mother bring the ultimate heartache: final rejection? Was I pre-judging what had happened in the past? Was I letting a fearful imagination cancel out contacting my mother? How could I know her thoughts? Maybe I had better leave well enough alone. And yet …

I rose from the bed and got my Bible. It had helped me before. I settled in a chair in the family room and snapped on a lamp. It gave me the inspiration I needed. I felt assured that seeking my mother was right.

Early the next Saturday morning, 18 January, I called. Two rings …

'Hello,' came a soft Southern voice.

My voice was uncharacteristically shaky for a news–announcer. 'Is this Clara?'

'Yes, it is.'

Suddenly I was tongue-tied. Finally I said, 'I love you.'

For a moment there was silence on the other end of the line. Then, 'I love you too. Who is this?'

'I … I think you know.'

A long pause, and then she asked, 'Is this Frankie?'

Three hours of non-stop talking filled in a lot of the gaps. I learned that my mother had been pregnant with me before she and my father got married. This had not set well with my strait-laced grandparents. Shortly after I was born my father left for the service. My mother, with nowhere else to go, stayed with my grandparents, who had little respect for her. Somehow they convinced the naive girl, little more than a child herself, that they could do a better job of raising me. The marriage was dissolved and she went off to find a new life. By the time my father returned from the war, she had married someone else.

'Oh, Frankie,' she cried, 'I never stopped thinking of you. I wanted to find you all these years, but I wasn't sure what you had been told. I was afraid you had been told I was dead.'

Mum went on to say that for some strange reason she felt a strong urge to find me about the same time my feeling about finding her intensified. The one thing that really inspired her search, she said, was the miraculous survival of her daughter-in-law in an airline crash.

'It was a sign from God,' she said. 'I felt that if he could save Vicki, He could help me find you.' Her daughter-in-law was Vicki Chavis, the stewardess whose story I had related on my radio newscast. I had been reporting on a sister-in-law I didn't know I had!

Mum went on to say she had long pressured my father for my address through the years. 'But he always felt it was better to leave things as they were,' she said. When she heard I was with a radio station somewhere, she had called every station in the country. She must have missed mine or reached someone there who didn't know me.

'Then this January my church newsletter dealt with the theme Let Go, Let God,' she continued. 'I made those words my own, Frankie. I figured I'd stop trying to make our reunion happen, and just let it happen. And now – ' She choked back a sob. 'And now it has!'

That was more than six years ago. Today I not only have regained my mother – a brown-eyed mother who loves me and wants me – but I also have three sisters and a brother. And the uncanny thing is that when I finally met them, it was as though I had known them all my life.

Yes, it took a long time – forty-two years. But our patience was rewarded. And today when I do my Mother's Day announcements over the air, it's hard to contain myself. You see, it's the happiest time of the year.

RETURN OF THE DUCKS

by Ardith Clarke

A child hopes against the odds.

Lorraine, her coat buttoned askew and her hat on backwards, was struggling into her new red boots.

'Where do you think you're going?' I asked.

'To the pond – to see if the ducks are back yet,' she said.

'We can see from here that they aren't. I don't think they are coming back, ever.' She looked at me, her eyes wide with disbelief. I tried to soften my words. 'I'm sure they've found another home by now. It must be a good one or they would not have strayed.'

She was too young to be burdened with facts about the helplessness of wild ducks whose wings have been clipped. The two ducks, named Mr Drake and Mrs Hen, had been extras in an experimental programme from my husband's work. He had brought them home hoping to shelter and feed them until the Autumn when they could forage for themselves and their feathers would be long enough for flight. Each morning he had carried them to a pen he had made for them at our pond and each night he had brought them in again.

One night the pen had been empty. Coyotes? Hunters? A half-starved dog we had seen loping across the field? The red-winged hawk that patrolled our meadow? We speculated about what had devoured our ducks. We knew they were dead, but we told Lorraine only that they were gone.

'I hope they aren't wet.' She had abandoned the boot project and was peering out the window, nose flattened against the pane.

'If they are out in this, they are wet. The whole world is wet – dripping, oozing wet.' Fog and mist had blanketed our world for days, hiding any glimmer of sunlight. Suddenly I felt very sorry for myself. Despair, like the mist, had blanketed my husband and myself for so long that there was little happiness left for us. No matter where I sent my thoughts, they could not penetrate the gloom engulfing me. The doctor had told us that because of complications in early pregnancy there was a chance our coming baby would he deformed.

'Will it have a defective mind or just a twisted little toe?' I had asked.

'No way to tell what the deformity is or even if there is one,' the doctor had said. 'All I can tell you is the statistic in a case like this is one-out-of-five chance for deformity.'

And so the statistic had become my ghostly companion, enfolding me like thick fog, seeping into my brain until not one part of my present or future was free of a feeling of impending disaster.

I sat down at the table with a cup of steaming tea and gazed out the window upon the barren fields of late Autumn, trying not to think. The pond that had teemed in the summer heat with ripples and sunshine lay bleak and lifeless in the clutches of approaching winter. The brown pool was as still as the barren fields beyond.

Then a shadow moved against the bank and a ripple of life streaked across the water. I grabbed the binoculars from the desk and focused. Mr Drake – our Mr Drake – his green head erect, glided elegantly across the water, at ease, at home, as though he had never been gone. Mrs Hen, her soft brown body almost indistinguishable from the muddy bank and water, was right beside him.

'The ducks are back!' I shouted. 'Get into your coat and boots. The ducks are back.' I forgot my stuffy nose, my ballooning stomach and statistics. All I could think about was serving the ducks a good-sized meal before they decided to go.

As I filled their pen with cracked grain, the ducks waddled up the far bank, loudly scolding my interruption. And as I watched their clumsy retreat, I marvelled that two fat, grounded mallards could strut around the countryside for ten days without being eaten or run over. What had been their chances of survival? One chance out of fifty? One out of a hundred? And if they did survive, what had been the chances of their returning to our little pond? One chance out of a hundred? One out of a thousand? Whatever the odds, I'm sure the statistics were against the ducks, but they had survived the statistics; they had returned.

'I knew they'd be back. I knew they'd be back,' Lorraine chanted, hopping on one foot and then the other. I smiled at her, knowing how easy it had been for her to believe in the ducks' return. She had not known the obstacles. She had never been filled with doubts.

Then, as always, my thoughts plunged inward again, but this time with different emphasis. I thought of my baby's statistics, my fears and apprehensions. I had dwelt on the one out of five chances for abnormality. Why had I lived in despair these past few months when I could have lived in hope? Even if the worst statistics became reality, an attitude of gloom would only deepen the tragedy, while faith might bring complete or partial healing – at the very least it would make the reality bearable. As I watched the ducks, I vowed to live on the sunny side of the statistical ledger, to always hope and expect the best.

The ducks' wings were feathered and strong for flight when I brought our baby home from the hospital. Even if Lou had not been nine pounds of health and wholeness, we would have loved her just the same. With hope, we would have done all possible to help her fulfil her potential.

To live on the sunny side of the ledger – this is the truth I learned the day the ducks came home.

TOTAL DARKNESS

by Bob Peters

After fifty years of life a blind man sees a beautiful, golden light.

I paused at the foot of the stairs, captured by the sound of my daughter's voice floating through the house as she sang and played piano in the living room. So beautiful, I thought. How I'd love to see the face that goes with that voice. But how does a man blind since birth picture a human face or a smile or eyes the colour of violets?

Robbie's song moved through me, stirring up the old longing that someday, somehow, I would be able to see her. In the beginning I'd yearned to watch her toddling with her first steps ... then, climbing out of the car on her way to school, then at graduation in her cap and gown. But all those moments had come and gone. Now as I listened to her – a young woman singing about love – I found myself with another longing. To see Robbie on her wedding day.

Shaking myself from the longings that her song roused, I made my way outside to wait for my driver, Debbie Epting, who'd take me to work. A bird twittered somewhere above me. I smiled at the sound, reminding myself that I'd never been gloomy about my blindness. I wasn't going to start now. I'd been blind all fifty years of my life. With my parents' help I'd learned to treat it more as a nuisance than a handicap. I'd worked my way through University, hitch-hiking eighteen miles back and forth to class each day, and making the dean's list.

It wasn't as if my blindness had sidelined me from life. I'd coached sports teams and even written and performed songs. And now after so many years of working for the YMCA, country clubs and leisure centres, I was preparing to open my own business as a professional masseur. I'd never been gloomy, it's true, but a million times and more I'd wished I could see my daughter.

The longing would come upon me at unexpected moments, like now, listening to Robbie's song. But not just Robbie. There was Ellie. How I ached for even a glimpse of the woman I'd married!

I had been born with scleroided corneas. Something I'd heard was beyond help from medical science, and long since I'd stopped going to doctors. I know my mother had prayed every day of my life that one day I would see. But I never prayed about it. I knew it was hopeless.

At last I heard Debbie's car pull alongside the kerb. I climbed in, summoning a cheerful hello, determined not to visit that gloomy place inside of me again.

The day moved forward. At noon Debbie sat down across the lunch table from me. 'You know,' she said, 'I think about you and your blindness a lot. How long has it been since you've seen a doctor?'

I turned my head towards her, touched by her concern, but almost amused at her naïveté. 'Believe me, Debbie, my condition is permanent.'

'How can you be so sure?' she asked.

'Because I've been told by doctors all my life, time and time again, that absolutely nothing can be done'

I didn't tell her how it had hurt to keep knocking on that door of hope and having it slammed in my face over and over. After a while I'd just quit knocking.

'But,' she persisted.

'Just forget it!' I interrupted, louder than I'd intended. I lowered my voice. 'Please.'

I could hear her finishing her lunch in silence, her fork scraping aimlessly across her plate. I returned to my meal, glad I'd put a cork on that useless idea. But just before I sealed the thought away completely, there it was again, like a puff of genie smoke escaping from a bottle – the longing to one day see the faces of my wife and family.

I forgot the little incident. Debbie, however, did not. In the days that followed, for reasons I couldn't begin to understand, she kept insisting I see a doctor. Why was she so compelled to keep badgering me when I kept resisting so firmly? The more she persisted, the more stubborn I became. Permanent blindness meant just that – permanent. I'd accepted my condition and made a good life for myself. It seemed better to concentrate on that.

A week passed. One morning, as she was driving me to my office, Debbie suddenly said, 'I need to stop by my optometrist's office to get my lenses cleaned. It won't take a minute.'

That struck me as a rather unusual thing to do on the way to work. But instead of questioning it I nodded. The last thing I wanted was more talk about eye doctors.

As she parked the car, I heard her take a long, deep breath, like a cautious sigh. 'Okay, we're here. And ... well, I've made an appointment for you too.'

I exploded. 'You did what?'

'Listen,' she said, 'why not just give it a try, it ...'

'But I've already tried, years ago, and I'm tired of having that door slammed in my face.'

'Bob,' she said firmly, 'I remember the time you said you'd give anything just to be able to see Ellie and Robbie. Did you really mean that, or were you just saying it?'

'I, I – ' Debbie had caught me off balance. I couldn't answer.

In a softer tone Debbie said, 'Please, just try it, for me. We're already here, and it won't take that long. Please come in with me.'

For the first time in seventeen years, almost two decades after giving up on ever seeing, I walked reluctantly into the office of an eye doctor.

Debbie was wrong about one thing. The examination took an impossibly long time. Finally the doctor spoke. 'Mr Edens, I believe there is some real hope here. Have you heard of the corneal transplants being done today?'

I listened as the doctor described advances in eye surgery. Advances I hadn't bothered to check, had almost stubbornly refused to hear about because I knew they would do me no good. I felt Debbie's hand on my shoulder. And for the first time in nearly twenty years I felt a flicker of hope.

Before I left that office that day I had agreed to try for a corneal transplant, but still I could not allow myself to believe it could happen. It seemed to me there was a needle-in-a-haystack possibility of finding an eye donor who matched my blood and tissue types. And even if that happened there was still no assurance the operation would be a success. The doctor wasn't confident either, but he assured me there was a chance, a good one.

The call came one brisk morning in Autumn over a year after that first visit. The hospital had found a donor and was on standby for my surgery. I left immediately. Ellie did not come with me. She was not well. Robbie, too, stayed home, to look after her mother.

The night before the operation I lay in my hospital bed, thinking, wondering what it might be like to see … to see a world I'd tried so hard to imagine through my ears and fingers. Oh, God, I said to Him, for so long I thought my wish was beyond you …

Once I'd heard a story from the Bible about a man blind since birth. One day Jesus met him on a Jerusalem street and gave him his sight. I'd always thought things like that only happened in the pages of the Bible. But now I was ready to do what Debbie had urged – to stop wishing and to start hoping. Suddenly the words my mother had always prayed were there inside me too: 'Please God, tomorrow, let me see.'

When the next day came I had the operation, then lingered for hours in post-operative sleep. It was the middle of the night before I finally woke up. I could feel the gauze taped across my eyes. I heard my brother Pete talking quietly in the room with his wife.

Then I heard the clicking sound of a lamp being turned on. Suddenly, to my astonishment, I became aware of something reaching through the bandages, something startlingly strange. My breath lodged in my chest. I searched for my voice.

'Pete, did you just turn on a light?' I asked.

'Yes, but ... how did you know?'

I tried to curb the flood of excitement rising in me. That was light filtering through the bandages. Beautiful, golden light! My hand reached up to touch the bandage. 'I can tell there is light coming from somewhere!'

Pete said maybe it was just a reaction to the surgery, or perhaps my imagination. I knew he didn't want me to get my hopes up too soon. 'Just wait till they remove the bandages,' he said.

For the longest time I lay there savouring that small, faint ray of light that came so gently through the bandage. Was it my imagination?

In the early hours of the morning a nurse came to my bedside rattling a medicine tray. She began matter-of-factly to pull the adhesive and gauze away from my face. 'Now, Mr Edens, open your eyes,' she said. 'I need to drop in some medicine.'

Slowly my eyes opened into a world full of light, dazzling light. And there, dangling over my eyes I saw the exquisite form of a tiny glass eye dropper. It was beautiful.

I blinked and looked up into the nurse's face bent next to mine. She was the first human being I'd ever seen. And she was beautiful, too.

The room seemed to hang in silent wonder. I turned my head. My vision fell on a most splendid thing sitting on the bedside table. Why this is a flower, I thought. The colour was so brilliant, it seemed to be alive and pulsing. It was a poinsettia.

I lay back on my pillow. 'Oh, dear God, thank you. Thank you ... thank you.'

After a few weeks of convalescence, I returned home anxious to see – to see – my family. As I approached the front door, it burst open. There in the doorway was a lovely young woman with shining blue eyes and a smile that seemed to circle her face. 'Daddy!' she cried.

I reached out and hugged her to me. Then I saw Ellie. For a suspended moment I stared into her marvellous face. Then my arms went around her too.

My days are different now. Very different. Can you imagine what it's like to wake up every morning and see something for the first time, like little purple flowers poking through a pathway, or the sun painting the clouds pink? It's hard to believe how much colour and beauty and movement God has packed into the world – grass after rain, a squirrel running up a tree, a gaudy October leaf. And can you imagine how I felt when I saw my daughter's blue eyes behind her snowy wedding veil?

But gaining my eyesight has only been part of a larger change in me that started just before that first eye examination. As I marvel at life's daily parade of wonders, I think how blessed I was to have had Debbie come into my life and spark that first flicker of hope in me. I am a deeper person, and my faith in God is deeper, for now I know why wise men tell us that we human beings should never, ever give up hope.

Looking back I know now that for most of my years I did not know what hope was – I spent my time wishing for sight, not really hoping for it. A hope is stronger than a wish; it is the feeling that the thing we wish for will happen. It is the beginning of belief – of faith. And when we believe, we know for certain that anything can happen!

4

WHEN LONELINESS IS CONQUERED

Since the death of my husband, I have known lonely moments. However, I refuse to let them build into lonely days. Work, reaching out to others, and trusting in the close presence of God have helped me to knock loneliness on the head.

Wendy Craig

THE MANY SHAPES OF LONELINESS

by Maureen O'Sullivan

How one woman resolved one of life's perpetual problems.

In 1963 my husband, John Farrow, died. We had been married twenty-six years and were the parents of seven children. I was very fortunate, I believe, in having a career which I could resume, an acting career. Aside from financial necessity and the fact that I do enjoy acting, it was good to be busy. That's the advice everyone gives a new widow: 'Stay busy.'

In this case, 'everyone' is right. It is wise to be very busy. But a full schedule does not stop you from thinking back and it does not prevent that underlying sense of sadness from gnawing at you. Like wind in a rustic cabin, it comes through the chinks of living, at unexpected moments and places. It is generally some tiny thing that triggers the melancholy – something you want to share and suddenly you are surprised that he's no longer there. Certain things force you to remember because you no longer know how to accomplish them; how to order plane tickets, for instance. John always did that for me. And there's that painful moment when you go into a restaurant alone and ask for a table. I'm convinced that the rule for a restaurant is the same as that for the Ark: You appear only in pairs.

These things, however, are mere scratches. They come nowhere near the depths of that great yearning thing, that 'shuffling of memory and desire', that ageless hunger we call loneliness. I have been lonely many times during my lifetime – who has not been? – but it is only in the last several years that I have been able to determine the many shapes of loneliness. There are a number of them.

Certainly Christmas Day, my first year in Hollywood, represented one shape. I was eighteen, fresh from Ireland, waiting to do my first (of five) Tarzan pictures (no matter my other roles, I seem to be remembered as 'Tarzan's Jane'). I was alone that Christmas, and feeling the early tinges of self-pity.

I thought of my mother far away in Ireland. As a widow, her own advice about loneliness had always been 'Contact someone'. She meant really contact, to learn as much as possible about that person, to understand, to help. 'Stretch a hand to one unfriended and thy loneliness is ended.'

But my mother was outgoing; I was not, nor was I quick to make friends. What worked for her, and well, would not necessarily work for me.

As it turned out, that Christmas Day was a most successful one because I used my aloneness for a purpose.

Years later, in reading Anne Morrow Lindbergh's *Gift from the Sea,* I was reminded of that purpose:

'For it is not physical solitude that actually separates one from others,' Mrs Lindbergh wrote, 'not physical isolation, but spiritual isolation. It is not the desert island nor the stony wilderness that cuts you from the people you love. It's the wilderness in the mind, the desert wastes in the heart through which one wanders lost and a stranger. When one is estranged to oneself, then one is estranged from others, too. If one is out of touch with oneself, then one cannot touch others.'

That day I began to look at myself. I made certain that my goals were worthy ones and natural to me. And I drew confidence from confirming the fact that the career that lay in challenge was something I could and should undertake. So it happened that, as I made the effort to get in touch with myself, my loneliness dissolved. But that was only one kind of loneliness. There were others.

There was The War. John was away in the Navy. Everyone was doing something helpful. I was volunteering at St John's Hospital and being mother and temporary father to the children. The days were full and often frantic, but after nine o'clock in the evening, with the children tucked into bed and the house silent, I'd face the night hours and shiver.

It is true that children, with their lives to be fashioned and their problems to be solved, can absorb you. Children can fill a home to the tiptop, but John's absence could not be camouflaged by activity. Night after night I'd find myself restlessly roaming the house, *Is this,* I wondered, *what being a widow is like?* I didn't know until later that true widowhood is a loneliness of a different texture.

In wartime, one lives closer to God. And for a while I thought that my restlessness would become easier through prayer. Instead, it seemed to grow more acute. Perhaps prayers for myself are wrong, I thought, though I knew at heart that any communion with God must be in some way beneficial. Yet, I also knew that the answer to my problem would come eventually from a realisation within myself. It did, in an oblique way.

A friend of mine's baby was stillborn. Later, she and I talked about the tragedy and its meaning and, at one point, she said to me, 'If I had known ahead of time that my baby were to be born dead, I believe the physical pain of birth would have been unendurable. It's odd about pain, isn't it? If there's good reason for it, you endure it – sometimes gladly.'

The curious thing was that I took my friend's thought about pain and applied it to my own problem. A philosopher once wrote, 'He who has a why to live for can bear almost any how.' Aware that I did indeed have a 'why' – John's return – I now knew that I could and would endure the 'how' – loneliness. This loneliness, I said, is my own special, personal, private participation in the war. I was able to put my loneliness in perspective when I was able to say, 'I will endure it. John will come home.' And he did.

There came a time, though, when I no longer had that perspective. The ache I felt was different from the previous aches. It was deeper, emptier. My husband was dead; the 'why' gone. This was the texture of true widowhood – emptiness.

The children were older now and, for the most part, busy with their own projects and careers from which I was excluded. That was as it should have been.

It seemed wrong to be lonely. My career went well. I was starring in a Broadway play *Never Too Late*, and it was a great hit. I went out often. I knew that the life of an actress, a celebrity-type, had an advantage over the widow who lived within a small circle in a quiet town. Yes, of course it had, except that when I returned home, the contrast was shattering.

That is when I began to re-evaluate loneliness, to review its previous forms, to bring logic and heart and faith to bear. I drew some conclusions which I hold now. Perhaps those conclusions are not the ones that people suffering from loneliness want to hear, but I believe they are basic and true.

Most of us, I fear, do not wish to face the fact that human beings are lonely creatures. We have been lonely always; we will be always. I am not being flippant when I say that the one area in which we are not alone is our loneliness. Everywhere I go I find people who are lonely and for whom there seems to be no relief or answer. Certainly as a woman I recognise that there is a restlessness in me that is not satisfied by human contact or by a full schedule.

It has been said that loneliness is a searching for God. Centuries ago, St Augustine wrote, 'Thou hast made us for Thyself, and restless are our hearts until they rest in Thee.' Yes, we are born searching and restless and only when we can admit the hard fact that we are lonely, and will remain so, is there hope for some tranquillity and receptivity to life. It is then that we can begin to appreciate the world that God created for us to accept and use, not deny.

In the play *The Chalk Garden* by Enid Bagnold, there is a governess who has had a particularly ill-starred life. When yet another misfortune befalls her which seems to close off her future, she is asked what she plans to do. Her answer: 'I shall continue to explore the astonishment of living.'

Life is astonishing. Not just in its vastness, but in the microscopic too, in its infinite, intriguing details and in what many of us condemn as routine and day-to-day. But be aware of today, to know that it is different from yesterday and to welcome the adventure of tomorrow is to accept life. To accept life is to remove the pain from loneliness.

BASIC TRAINING

by Vickie Aldous

I had never felt further from God in my whole life.

It was Sunday morning, and as the lights flooded the barracks for wake-up, my only wish was to be back home safely in bed.

How did I ever get into this? I asked myself as I crawled from beneath my woollen blanket. I wondered if any of the other fifty girls in my squad were as tired as I was.

I remembered my junior school and my first visit with the Army recruiter. He told me how I could join the Reserves and earn money to help pay for college. All I had to do was complete two months of basic training in the summer. When I graduated from secondary school, I would spend another summer in advanced training, and then serve weekend drills near my home.

It seemed perfect. How hard could two months of basic be? I knew I could survive anything for that length of time.

Now, as I made my bed with perfect, squared corners, I wasn't so sure.

I had always considered myself physically fit, but the Army's idea of physically fit was entirely different. Each day we got up at 4 a.m. to exercise. The routines alternated: One morning we did sit-ups and push-ups, and the next we ran anywhere from three to four-and-a-half miles. This was called PT, which stood for 'physical training'. To me the initials meant 'prolonged torture'.

I had run cross-country and track at school, so the run was not too difficult for me. The sit-ups and push-ups were something else, though. Only a week into basic I was so sore that I could barely move. My shoulders cramped from activities as simple as lifting a fork during a meal. Whenever I laughed, which wasn't often, my stomach muscles ached.

Often during the predawn darkness of PT I looked up at the stars from the sit-up position and wondered if there really was a God up there.

None of us was used to being yelled at by drill sergeant night and day for anything, no matter how trivial, done wrong. Many were away from home for the first time. There was virtually no privacy, and we received, on average, about five hours of sleep each night.

The biggest taboo of all was to break down and cry. The few people who allowed tears to fall were branded as cry-babies.

We were constantly on edge and irritated with one another. I had always got along fairly well with people and rarely lost my temper. But now I found myself restraining an impulse to strangle people.

Our drill sergeants could plainly see our lack of camaraderie and they used it against us. Whenever an individual made a mistake, we all paid. Dropping and doing push-ups because someone twitched at the wrong moment did not exactly endear that person to the rest of the squad.

Of course, the army had its own logic for this system. It fostered peer pressure to always do the right thing, even when the drill sergeant's back was turned.

Everyone was pitted against everyone else. We became our own police force.

This morning was no different, even if it was Sunday. It was supposed to be our day off, but the reality was something else. We had to scrub the barracks spotlessly clean from top to bottom. In addition, every Sunday our section was charged with mowing and raking an area of lawn as large as a football field.

As I got dressed I noticed that the fighting and bickering were already under way. People were arguing over who would get the morning shifts for lawn duty. It was better to do it in the relative cool of morning than wait and be out working under the blazing afternoon summer sun.

I went around the squabbling groups and put my name on the afternoon list. I wanted to go to church that morning. Devotion to God wasn't my only reason. I just didn't feel like fighting my way through all those people. Also, this was about my only chance for some peace and quiet, and I intended to take advantage of it.

The church was filled to its capacity of about four hundred people. I sat in a pew with about ten other girls, and we all listened politely as the sermon began. The chaplain wasn't very enthusiastic. It was his fourth service of the morning, and he was probably worn out. His subject was generic – about keeping God in sight when faced with adversity. Instead of inspiring me, it only emphasised my feelings of isolation. I felt all alone, even though I was surrounded by Christians. Why couldn't God show me He still loved me – now when I needed Him most?

The chaplain's message ended and he asked if anyone had anything to share. We all sat in silence, until a girl stood up.

'I would like to sing a song I wrote,' she said nervously.

I was surprised. Nothing would have convinced me to talk in front of all those people, let alone sing. I admired her for it.

Her first simple words went straight to my heart:

God, I'm feeling so alone
In this place so far from home.
Please listen to this prayer
And show me you still care.

Here was someone going through the same thing I was! Her words were sure and beautiful now as she went on with the song, and every verse echoed my own secret thoughts. Now I knew I wasn't the only one who felt so isolated, but I still didn't understand how God could have abandoned us.

Suddenly I was overwhelmed with self-pity, and tears welled up in my eyes. Dear God, I prayed, please don't let me cry in front of all these people!

I glanced around furtively to see if anyone had noticed. To my surprise, everyone around me was fighting back tears too! I looked up and didn't even bother to wipe my tears away. 'Hey, you guys,' I whispered, 'we're not alone. We have one another.'

For a few seconds, we looked around dazedly as the realisation slowly dawned on us. It was as if we all were looking beyond the tough outsides and fighting to see the potential friends in front of us. We had been so busy trying to hide our feelings, we didn't even realise others felt the same way.

That's when we all broke down. Everyone was hugging one another, smiling and crying at the same time.

Then the girl who had started all this finished her song:

How could I have been so blind?
Why did it take so long to find?
Your love's before my eyes,
In the friends that you supply.

As she sat down, the rest of us stood up, clapping. All around our small group, row by row, people got to their feet. Soon the whole church was giving her a standing ovation.

With a simple song, God had shown us that He was still there, and He loved us.

Maybe it wasn't so simple, after all.

THE DAY I BECAME A NEIGHBOUR

by Marion McClintock

The wave that brought life to an unknown man.

Some years ago my husband, Earl, and our two young children moved house. I resented the move; it was a wrench to leave my family and friends. Worse, we'd put all our furniture in storage and had rented a small, furnished house in a nondescript neighbour-hood near Earl's new job.

The furniture was a motley array of unmatched pieces, nicked and scratched by former users, and would not respond to my vigorous cleaning and polishing.

But my greatest desolation was my utter loneliness. I would sit for hours and cry.

Earl suggested I make friends with the neighbourhood women. But I was so homesick that I shrank within a wall around myself.

When Earl spoke of inviting people from his office for a visit, I said no. I was ashamed for anyone to see our home.

Another thing about the house that bothered me was the constant presence of flies and other bugs. I sprayed and swatted them all over the house. Whenever I went out of or came in the house, I always stopped at the door and waved away any flying creatures that might be lurking nearby.

At the end of our street was a house with a porch where an elderly man sat for most of the day. I guessed he was ill.

One day my doorbell rang. I hastily removed my apron and ran into the bedroom to smooth my hair and powder my nose. 'It's probably just a door-to-door salesman,' I told myself, but I was determined to present myself as a proper 'lady of the house'.

The forlorn-looking woman on my steps was not selling anything. Her hair was disarrayed, her clothes hung loosely on her, and her eyes were red and swollen from weeping. She looked familiar.

'Come in,' I said. 'Please sit down.' While she was seating herself, I quickly whisked a small rug over the worn place in the carpet.

'I'm sorry to bother you,' she said, twisting a damp ball of handkerchief in her lap. 'I wouldn't have the nerve to ask you this, but I know you were always so friendly to my father.'

I got up and turned off the radio so she couldn't see my startled look.

'Your father?' I managed to say.

'Oh, I'm sorry,' she replied. 'I guess you didn't know. He passed away last night.' She fought back tears.

'My father,' she went on, 'was lonely in his last days. He did not know many people here. We came here from a town where we knew everyone and they knew us. You'll never know how much it meant to him to have you wave when you went in and out of your door. But he couldn't wave back. His arms were paralysed.'

Tears of shame rolled down my cheeks at the undeserved tribute. Then she asked if she could borrow a black coat she had seen me wearing. She wanted to wear it to her father's funeral. I eagerly got it for her.

When she left, I knew that I had reached a turning point. My self-pity and self-centredness were the real causes of my loneliness. I knew now that I had to make the first move, the first overture to friendship.

That night I greeted Earl at the door with a smile and even overlooked the dirt the children tracked in behind him.

The next day I joined the other neighbours in providing home-cooked meals for the bereaved family. A few days later, when I learned a young housewife on our block was expecting her first baby, I gave a party for her at our home and invited all the other women on the block. No one seemed to notice the old furniture – nor did I anymore.

Months later we moved to another part of town. But this time there was no loneliness, no depressing period of adjustment. For I remembered the lesson I had learned from the old gentleman who mistook my angry arm waving for an act of friendliness.

This time it was no mistake – my greetings really were friendly. And I again found good neighbours by being one.

BEYOND THE WALL

by Cheryl Urow

The bricks that linked one lonely girl to her world-wide family.

I was travelling in Israel with a group of forty other teenagers. It was the fourth day of touring and I sat towards the back of our bus, alone, feeling very sorry for myself. I had hoped to meet new, interesting people – maybe make lifetime friendships – but most of the students in our group seemed to be travelling with their own friends from home. Getting acquainted wasn't as easy as I thought it would be. And our guide that day spoke only Hebrew! I couldn't understand most of what he said. None of the others understood him either, but they were managing to have fun. Up front, a cluster of them were singing and laughing. I longed to be one of them. Instead I slumped in my seat, staring out the window.

Just then the guide announced a stop. I envisioned him leading us to yet another historical sight whose significance I wouldn't grasp because it would be explained all in Hebrew. And I saw myself standing alone in the crowd. My gloominess increased.

The bus lurched to a halt and we all piled out. I shuffled along with the rest, not paying much attention, until I saw the guide gesturing vigorously to the left.

I turned – and drew a quick breath.

What I saw didn't need an explanation. I knew it well from pictures. It was the Wailing Wall, the Western Wall. This wall in Jerusalem is the only remnant left standing of the Holy Temple –

the religious centre of Jewish life in ancient times, a sacred part of Jewish history, a terminus for Jewish pilgrims.

Slowly, reverently, I walked towards it and, when I was close enough, reached out and touched the stones. The effect was immediate, electric. I felt as if I touched all Jews throughout the world and throughout history. I was one with every Jew who had come to pray here.

The Wall had withstood time, weather, war. So, too, had the Jewish people, my people.

Suddenly I began to laugh at myself. Minutes earlier I'd been overwhelmed by feelings of isolation and aloneness, shut off behind a barrier of self-pity. Now I felt linked to millions – closer to all Jews, to the God we shared, to my heritage of faith. And all thanks to this good, strong wall, this wall of faith. It was the only kind of wall I wanted in my life.

Now I knew what to do about my lonely feelings. I turned to the girl beside me.

'Hi,' I said, and I gave her a big smile.

THE GIRL WHO EXCELS

by Ivy Coffey

A woman astronaut defies isolation.

How would anybody 'excel in loneliness'? Yet that's the way a city psychiatrist described Jerrie Cobb.

I may know the answer. Jerrie and I are friends. We share a rambling old eight-room house and are co-owners of a black-and-tan dachshund named Puppchen.

On a cold September morning Jerrie, who is thirty and who has been flying planes since she was twelve, entered a special laboratory in the Veterans Administration hospital here. She was about to undergo a test, the culmination of months of rigorous physical and psychological examinations given to determine whether she was fit for space travel. This was called the 'isolation' or 'sensory deprivation' test.

Jerrie was wearing the bathing suit she had been instructed to put on. She knew nothing about what lay ahead.

'You may terminate the test at any time,' Jerrie was assured by the scientists in charge. 'We shall be listening for your signal.'

Then Jerrie entered a tank, a blacked-out, claustrophobic cylinder in which she lay afloat in a pool of warm water. There was nothing else to touch or hear or taste; she could see nothing, smell nothing.

It is a fact that 90 per cent of the people who take this test end by having hallucinations. These people cannot stand the isolation from the world any more than they can bear being alone with themselves.

A staff listened electronically to Jerrie's every breath. When she talked, she was not answered. The minutes ticked into an hour. Jerrie could be heard napping for a few minutes. Two hours went by and Jerrie's reactions were the same as they had been in the first hour. More hours passed. Jerrie took two naps of about six minutes each. Finally, Jerrie heard a voice saying:

'There's no need for you to stay in any longer, Jerrie.'

Later, Jerrie was told that it was needless for her to have continued longer because her reactions hadn't changed; there was nothing else to be learned.

'How long do you think you were in there?' a doctor asked.

Jerrie thought carefully. 'About four-and-a-half hours,' she replied. She had been in that suspended, near weightless state for nine hours and forty minutes.

Jerrie did pass, and brilliantly, the extensive series of examinations. Simultaneously it was revealed that female astronauts may have advantages over men: they have lower body mass, use much less oxygen and need less food, hence may be able to go up in lighter capsules and stay up longer. But still, the important qualifications for rocket fitness have little to do with being male or female, and from Jerrie I have discovered that the quality most essential to the astronaut is a quality just as available to you and to me.

It was after the tests that the Veterans Administration psychiatrist, Dr Jay T. Shurley, made his statement: 'She's a girl who excels in loneliness.'

That's a phrase worth remembering. Nowadays, when I think of the countless people who complain of loneliness, of empty lives, I think of Jerrie. She came out of the cylinder with a keener appreciation of colour and texture and even noise, but the important thing was that she had not been lost when these ordinary things had been removed from her. How many people fail to cope with life even when they have their full complement of senses?

One time, in her mild, quiet way, Jerrie mentioned that the isolation test had been a 'pleasant state' for her. And then she said, 'When they take everything from you, there is still faith. That's what's left and that's enough.'

Jerrie's faith impressed Dr Shurley too. 'There is no doubt,' he said, 'that Jerrie's faith in God was of help in meeting the demands of isolation. She knew she had nothing to fear and so she could be alone in security. It is a matter of trust.'

But how does one get such a firm belief? It would be difficult to find out by asking Jerrie, for hers is not an ostentatious faith. She does not talk about it freely. But I have seen her during a relaxed day at home when she has slipped away to her den upstairs. It's a room filled with trophies and souvenirs, but its focal point is a charcoal grey altar over which is suspended a crude ebony crucifix which Jerrie brought back from South Africa. Here, on a thick white llama rug from Peru, Jerrie kneels and communes with God.

If she were to suggest how she had acquired her faith, I think she might say that it was as simple a matter as recognising and believing, totally, in God. Yet, I have heard her tell how, for years, hers was an immature faith that had to be nurtured by experience. There was even a time when she lost interest in God.

Her great love was always aeroplanes. Her father, an Air Force captain, started teaching Jerrie to fly when she was twelve. Her teens were spent around airstrips; she worked hard waxing planes and doing arduous chores to earn enough money for air time. Later she taught at a flying school. There were jobs, too, as a charter pilot, flying a pipeline patrol and crop spraying, and eventually ferrying planes to South America. One day, while en route to Lima, Peru, delivering a T–6 single engine plane to the Peruvian Air Force, she had one of the most important experiences of her life.

Flying alongside her in another T–6 was her boss. They landed at Esmeraldas, Ecuador, to refuel. Ahead were low clouds, rain, patches of fog. No real weather information was available at this small Indian village airstrip, so Jerrie's boss made the decision to fly on to Quayaquil, Ecuador. They flew under the overcast fifty feet above the jungle. The Andes loomed ahead, when, suddenly, a wild rainstorm lashed in.

Jerrie's boss signalled for her to climb up through the overcast; then he disappeared. But Jerrie was not an instrument pilot and had no training for flying blind.

'I could see nothing but the grey void all about me,' she wrote later. 'It was like being suspended in a huge bottle of milk. I had no sense of which way was up or down and I was frozen with panic.'

It had been three years since her last, ill-chosen attempt at prayer. So why should God bother to help her now? After all, she had rejected Him. Yet in this supreme moment of helplessness she knew that God was the only hope she now had. With all her heart, she put her life into His hands.

Jerrie has no explanation for what then happened. She does not remember manoeuvring the plane except to keep it from stalling. Yet a few minutes later she broke into sunshine and blue sky. Checking her compass, she found the plane had made an 80-degree turn; it was heading in the opposite direction from Quayaquil. Quickly she turned back on course.

Two hours later Jerrie landed. Her very worried boss met her, began firing questions. When Jerrie told him her course after climbing on top of the clouds, he replied, 'You know the trick, then.'

'What trick?'

Then he told her how, when climbing through clouds near mountains, a pilot should always make an 80-degree turn until he is on top of the clouds. Thus, by turning back over the course just travelled, he minimises the chance of flying into a mountain.

Jerrie had not known about this. Yet this is the course her plane took.

Since that adventure, Jerrie's life has been different. She has felt a confidence, a security, an extra inner resource which relates directly, I think, to her qualifications as an astronaut.

I know many things about Jerrie – that she likes mashed potato sandwiches for breakfast, is afraid of grasshoppers (but that's all), has a deep dimple on her left cheek, and that she would much prefer to fly over jungles and hazardous mountains than make a speech. She likes to cook (particularly Chickasaw Indian dishes), enjoys social dating (no serious romances so far) and prefers flying with her shoes off.

But what I know most is that Jerrie is eager to make that space flight, and she continues to prepare herself for that eventuality. The demands it makes she will be equal to – aloneness and loneliness cannot disturb her – Jerrie knows God's presence.

WHEN WORDS
ARE NOT ENOUGH

by Marjorie Willsie

Saying it with a hug.

I recently called on a new neighbour and allotted myself ten minutes for the call, just long enough, I thought, to invite her children to the local community party and make her feel welcome.

Something she said, though, revealed a common interest and we were off. Two hours had passed when I finally decided that I really must leave. Instead of shaking hands at the door, she impulsively threw her arms about me and gave me a big hug. 'Oh,' she laughed, 'I'm so glad you stopped. You have no idea how lonely I've been!'

Until that moment I had not realised how lonely I was. I have a fine family and wonderful neighbours. Why should I feel lonely?

Thinking about it on the way home, I realised that none of my many friends had ever made such a spontaneous show of affection towards me. I knew they liked me, maybe even loved me, and I was certain of their loyalty to me, but none had ever hugged me.

I felt a bond with Joyce, whom I had just met, that was stronger than the friendship I felt for my other friends, and it was wonderful to feel appreciated!

The whole episode kept running through my mind. It started me thinking about the very special times in my life when people had reached out to me and given me strength, courage or comfort by just a touch. I wondered why we are so reluctant to show emotion. Why not bestow a hug, a pat on the back, or a sympathetic touch without fear of seeming silly?

There was the time years ago when our second child announced he was on his way. The room was cold and the night seemed unbearably long. The doctor had come and gone, remarking as he left that it was probably a false alarm. I watched my mother-in-law as she moved about the room stuffing rags in the cracks around the window, filling the old wood stove, keeping busy. I was not particularly close to her and, as I huddled by the fire, I felt all alone in my own miserable little world.

I closed my eyes and a tear rolled down my cheek, followed by many others. I let them roll.

Then something exceptional happened. My mother-in-law stopped, laid her arm across my shoulder and, without a word, hugged me briefly to her. As she resumed her chores I knew of a certainty that I was not alone any more. That hug told me that there was someone who knew how I felt and who cared. A couple of hours later, with our new son snuggled beside me, I fell asleep still feeling the warmth of that hug.

Mothers are always hugging their little ones, and the children hug back, don't they? But what about the kids who are taller than their mothers? Hugging one's mother is not cool or something, and she doesn't hug them because she is afraid of offending them.

There was the time my eighteen-year-old son was leaving to work in another part of the country. I drove him to a friend's house where he was to get his lift. I felt like he was going to another world. With moist eyes I watched them load his things into his friend's car; then suddenly everyone went into the house and left me standing there.

He had not said good-bye.

I waited until the tears began to spill down my cheeks too fast for me to wipe them away. I wasn't going to leave without saying good-bye, and I wasn't going to run in and embarrass him.

Suddenly he came running down the path. He drew me close to him and said, 'Mum, don't cry. I'll be careful and I'll be okay. I'll even write to you. Good-bye, Mum. Take care.' The feel of that hug still lingers, warm and firm, around my shoulders.

Another time, I lay in a hospital bed next to a woman named Norma who was racked with pain. For several days, while we shared that room, we talked, sometimes in the middle of the night while she waited for the shot to give her an hour or two of rest. She knew she was going to have to have more operations and much more pain. But after that there would be a chance to get more schooling, to learn a profession, and time to spend with her adopted son.

When I was ready to be discharged, I suddenly found myself with nothing to say. Simple words of cheer rang hollow, so I did the only thing that seemed right. Leaning down, I touched each shoulder as gently as I could and kissed her cheek. I knew that even a tender touch hurt her; but there was a bond of love and understanding there, and with it the faith that someday she would make her dreams come true.

There are times when money and gifts won't help and kind words sound flat and meaningless. Such a time may be the occasion when a hug or a touch of affection will be all you have to give. If so, give it unreservedly and feel the blessing go two ways.

LESSON FROM A PENGUIN

by Edmund Boyle

A traveller finds a cure for loneliness.

I've spent the majority of my career as a travelling salesman, and I know that much of a salesman's free time on the road is spent battling loneliness. There's not a sorrier bunch anywhere than a group of salesmen eating their lunches alone in a motorway service station, and their dinners in an impersonal hotel. But one year my little daughter, Jeanine, gave me the antidote for my homesickness.

It had black beady eyes, a red bow tie and orange feet – a stuffed toy penguin that stood about five inches tall. Attached to its left wing with paste (still wet when I tore away the wrapping) was a wooden sign bearing the hand-painted declaration, 'I Love My Dad!' I immediately granted it a place of honour on my dresser.

One morning when I was packing for a trip, I tossed the penguin in my suitcase. That night when I called home, Jeanine was distraught that the penguin had disappeared. 'Honey, it's here with me. I brought it on my trip.' That news pleased her considerably.

Henceforth the penguin came with me – as essential as my briefcase or shaving kit. And we made friends. I checked into my hotel, dumped out my bag and dashed to a meeting. When I returned, the maid had turned down the bed and propped the penguin on the pillow. In another hotel I found it perched in a fresh drinking glass on my bedside table (the penguin had trouble standing upright). The next morning I left it sitting in a chair. Again that night it was in the glass. I think these maids didn't want me to forget the penguin's message: I Love My Dad!

One night I discovered the penguin missing, and after a frantic phone call, I learned I had left it in my previous hotel room, where it had been rescued by a heroic maid. I drove a hundred miles to retrieve it, arriving near midnight. The penguin was waiting at the front desk. In the lobby, tired business travellers looked on at the reunion – I like to think with a touch of envy. One guy smiled and another shook my hand.

Once a bemused customs agent at the airport dug the penguin out of my suitcase and, holding it up, said, 'Thank goodness we don't charge a tax on love or you'd owe quite a bit!'

Jeanine is a college student now, and I don't travel as much. The penguin is back on my dresser. But it is still a reminder that love is a wonderful travelling companion. All those years on the road, it was the one thing I never left home without.

A WOMAN ALONE

by Kathryn Keller

She needed something stronger than her little blue pills to get over her grief.

A flash of red by our snow-covered barn caused me to catch my breath. For a moment I thought it was my husband, wearing his favourite flannel shirt. But it wasn't my husband, it was only a bird. Silently, I hated the creature for the memory it had provoked. Tears filled my eyes, and the bird – as though offended by my gaze – flew away.

It was winter, and my husband was dead. Three months ago he had suffered a heart attack while working around the buildings of our small dairy farm. He had been forty-two years old.

How long, I thought, will I continue to suffer this sense of loss? When will I ever be whole again? My husband's death had torn in my heart a gaping hole that refused to heal.

Numbly, I turned from the window and walked to the kitchen. While setting a place for lunch, I stared blankly at the single seam that cut across the centre of the table. Yesterday there had been two seams, but this morning I had removed the table's leaf and stored it in the cellar. With my husband gone, there was no need for the extra setting. How nice it would be, I thought bitterly, to be able to adjust to change as easily as this table – just snap together and carry on as usual. Again I felt the hot sting of tears. Never had I felt so alone.

My entire life had always revolved around my family, and now, it seemed, there was none. John, our twenty-two-year-old son, had recently received a promotion and been transferred halfway across the country. Shelley, our eighteen-year-old daughter, was away at school on the other side of the country.

'But Mum,' John had approached me after the funeral, 'I don't have to stay here. I don't like the idea of you being all alone. Considering the circumstances. I'm sure my boss will let me return to my old job, and I can come and live near you.'

'No,' I had replied firmly. 'This promotion is too important to your career for you to pass it by. Please don't worry about me. I'll be fine.'

About the same time, Shelley caught me alone in the family room.

'Really, Mother,' she said, 'I don't have to go back to college. Or I could transfer to a school closer to home.'

'No, you won't,' I said. 'You've had your heart set on college since you were a little girl. You're settled there now, and doing well. I think you should stay.'

Deep down inside I would have given anything if either one of the children could have stayed. But I knew they had their own lives to lead. It was important to let them go.

In the days following my husband's funeral, there had been much to do. But once the flurry of post-funeral activities ended, with each passing day I grew more and more depressed. I just couldn't get used to being a widow. I tried reading books on the subject, but they only seemed to heighten my sense of aloneness. When lunchtime came, I still half-expected to hear the creak of the back door opening, the sound of my husband stamping his muddy work boots on the mat. Gradually, my depression became so bad that I often chose not to answer the phone, and – except to buy groceries – I rarely left the house. Sometimes I watched television, but I never seemed to remember a thing I'd seen or heard. Not even my favourite pastimes – oil painting, needlepoint, long walks – appealed to me. I had neither energy nor interest.

When I wasn't depressed, I was angry. Anything that reminded me of my husband aroused my fury: our favourite song on the radio, a glimpse of the fir tree we had planted together when we bought the farm – even the calls and visits of well-meaning friends.

Most of all, I was angry at God. From the day of the funeral, I stopped going to church. I dropped out of the art classes. If God was indeed a personal God, then He was cruel and heartless. Otherwise, how could He have allowed my husband to die?

At the sound of the doorbell, I frowned with annoyance. Why couldn't people leave me alone? Quietly, I got up and peered through the peephole in the door. It was my neighbour Marcella. While other friends had stopped calling, Marcella was persistent. Not a week passed without her stopping by.

I opened the door.

'Kaye!' she exclaimed, with her cheery smile. 'Mind if I come in?'

'All right,' I said dully. 'I'm just fixing lunch.'

I made cheese on toast, and we sat at the kitchen table. After chatting for about ten minutes, Marcella became suddenly serious.

'Kaye,' she said, 'I'm worried about you. You've got to stop brooding. This can't go on forever, you know.'

'I know,' I said.

'Did you ever consider seeing a doctor?' she asked. 'You're under a lot of stress. Maybe he can give you something to help.'

I said nothing.

'Well, that does it,' said Marcella, reaching for the kitchen phone. 'I'm making an appointment for you right now What's your doctor's number?'

For some reason, I didn't resist. I gave Marcella the number and she made an appointment for the following morning.

The doctor prescribed tranquillisers, little blue pills. I was depressed, he explained, a natural reaction to the death of a loved one. The pills would help.

Used as prescribed, the pills did have a calming effect. They did nothing, however, to ease my heartache or loneliness. One day, just to see what would happen, I increased the dosage. It worked.

That is, like a sort of emotional Novocaine, it helped me to forget. As weeks passed by, I found myself having to increase the dosage still more to achieve the desired effect. My morning coffee was preceded by one pill, my afternoon tea by two, and another was needed at bedtime in order for me to sleep through the night. Occasionally I worried about the number of pills I was taking, but I talked myself out of any real fears. The pills made me feel better, I told myself. The doctor had prescribed them. Besides, I could stop taking them any time I wanted to.

Still, with five pharmacies in town, I staggered my visits to each so that no one would suspect my habit. All that was needed to renew the prescription was the label from the previous bottle.

The only time I didn't use the pills was when I was with my children. It wasn't that I didn't want them to know; rather, their company filled my loneliness to the extent that I didn't need the pills. When December arrived, the first anniversary of my husband's death, Shelley was able to spend her entire three-week Christmas vacation at home. It was wonderful. We shopped, laughed, had long talks and stayed up late watching television and eating popcorn. I never took a pill. But the morning of Shelley's departure, as I stood in the doorway and watched her car disappear down the road, I felt the hole in my heart reopen. Overwhelmed with loneliness, I reached for my pills. When two didn't work, I took two more.

This had been going on for about a month, when one day I woke to see Marcella kneeling beside me on the kitchen floor. Somehow, I managed to convince her that I had just had a dizzy spell. When she finally left me, I was gripped with fear greater than I'd ever known. Racing to the bathroom, I grabbed my bottle of pills and dumped them down the toilet. I was afraid to have them in the house, afraid I'd take too many again, afraid that next time there would be no one around to help. I may be depressed, I thought, as I tore the prescription label into tiny bits, but I'm not ready to die.

I also wasn't ready for what happened next.

In a matter of hours, I became violently ill. Trembling and nauseated, I was unable to eat or sleep. At some point it occurred to me that what I was suffering was withdrawal – I had read about it somewhere. For the first time since I started taking the pills, I was faced with the alarming fact that I had become an addict. As the evening went on, I didn't care. By morning my only concern was how to get more pills.

I knew I'd have to call the doctor and tell him I had lost my pre-scription. I panicked at the thought. What if he suspected? What if he said no? With a trembling hand, I dialled his number. A nurse took my message. Ten minutes later she called back to say the pharmacy had been notified; my pills were ready to be picked up.

After that, things got progressively worse. By early Spring, I was popping those little pills the way others eat mints. Somehow, I managed to put on a good front for friends, and for the children when they called.

But one afternoon as I stood with pill in one hand, glass of water in the other, a small thought – like a flashing traffic signal – seemed to say, Kath! Stop! This is your last chance! Now or never! There was such a sense of urgency and authority to the warning that it caused me to set the glass down.

And once again, I threw away my pills.

This time was worse than the last. By early evening, I began to shudder and shake. My head throbbed with pain. My body was racked with fever and chills. I spent the night a pathetic heap on the bathroom floor, clinging to the toilet bowl, retching and weep-ing. Devilish fears and tormenting anxieties caused me to cry out loud. Finally, I couldn't take it any longer.

'Please, God,' I sobbed, 'help me!' The next morning was Sun-day. I woke, chilled to the bone. I showered, and drank strong black coffee. I dressed and left the house. I would walk. I didn't know where, but I would walk. For some reason, I felt it was absolutely necessary that I leave the house. Besides, my husband and I had always taken our walks together. Arm-in-arm we often strolled across our property after an evening meal. On Sundays we walked to church. At the sound of organ music, I was surprised to see that that was where my walk had taken me on this Sunday morning. The service was about to begin; the sound of the music seemed to draw me closer. Just as the doors closed, I slipped into a back pew. Somehow it felt good to be in church, as though that was where I was supposed to be. At the same time I felt sad, though I didn't know exactly why. Emotionally spent, physically exhausted, I was acutely aware that I had sunk just about as low as a person could go. I thought about my addiction. I recalled the way I had spent my evening. I wondered what my husband would think. I started to cry.

'Father,' I prayed out of desperation more than anything else, 'please help me. If you're really there, set me free from these pills.'

I didn't really expect an answer. It has always been my understanding that approaching God in prayer required a person to have a lot of faith. I had very little. That's why I was surprised when – as if in direct response to my prayer – a kind of quiet reassurance came to me. 'I love you,' a voice seemed to say. 'Trust in me, and I will take care of you.'

The pain, the anger, the emptiness I had carried for so long were not removed, but somehow my capacity for endurance and struggle was increased. It was as though my words had put me in touch with a source of power and goodness and love unlike anything I'd ever known. And I knew that, sooner or later, I was going to be all right.

'Thank you, Father,' I murmured. 'Thank you.'

Not that the next few months were easy. At times the struggle seemed even worse.

More than once I was thrown to my knees in prayer when tempted to call the doctor for a new prescription. And for a long while I was ashamed to admit my battle with addiction to anyone but God.

All that changed, however, when one night I read in the Bible a passage from James 5:16: 'Pray for one another, that you may be healed.'

'Of course,' I cried out loud. 'Of course! You've been trying to do it all by yourself. You need the love and help that other people can give!'

The next day I confided my problem to Marcella and my children. Gaining their understanding, acceptance and prayerful support was probably the biggest step in my healing process.

Gradually, I began to adjust to life without my husband. I began to accept luncheon and dinner invitations from my friends. I rejoined the art classes and signed up for volunteer work at a local hospital and nursing home. On a few occasions, I found myself with the opportunity to comfort a grieving widow.

Today, though I still miss my husband terribly, I'm living a life more fulfilling and abundant than I ever would have dreamed possible! I have learned that there is no earthly substitute for a loved one who has died. But there is God. I know now that all the time He was waiting for me with a special kind of relationship more loving and enduring than any I had ever known. All I had to do was ask.

5

WHEN FAITH
HOLDS ON

*There have been many times when my faith
has been tested. I have to keep reminding myself
at such moments to keep trusting, and I'm always
so thankful that God honours my faith
and carries me through.*

Wendy Craig

MY FATHER'S SUCCESS

by William Hammerstein

The secret strength behind the famous lyricist.

His timeless lyrics told us to chase our dreams and never lose hope. Yet failure, for Oscar Hammerstein, was often a great teacher. Fifty years ago on 31 March, *Oklahoma!* America's first folk musical, opened on Broadway to critical and popular acclaim of historic proportions. The show became more than the talk of the town. Word soon spread throughout the country that in *Oklahoma!* composer Richard Rodgers and my father, lyricist Oscar Hammerstein II, had created something important and enduring, and uniquely American.

But Dad was not one to take success for granted; there had been years of struggle and disappointment. So at the end of 1943 he bought a full-page ad in the weekly show business trade publication *Variety* and publicly listed some of his theatrical flops:

Holiday Greetings
OSCAR HAMMERSTEIN, II
author of
Sunny River
(Six Weeks at the St James Theatre, New York)
Very Warm For May
(Seven Weeks at the Alvin Theatre, New York)
Three Sisters
(Six Weeks at the Drury Lane, London)

Ball At The Savoy
(Five Weeks at the Drury Lane, London)
Free For All
(Three Weeks at the Manhattan Theatre, New York)
I'VE DONE IT BEFORE AND I CAN DO IT AGAIN.

The ad was an exercise in humility. My father was reminding himself as much as anyone else that failure is often a wiser teacher than success. From each setback he had learned something valuable. Once on an opening night early in his career Dad knew almost the minute the curtain went up that the show he'd written would close. Yet that same night he started work on his next libretto.

Back in 1927 when *Show Boat* opened with Dad's lyrics and Jerome Kern's music, it was hailed as America's greatest operetta. The movies beckoned and Dad answered the call. He had not written for the screen before. He was unhappy on the West Coast and never did fit into the cut-throat Hollywood scene. After four years he returned east only to spend a dozen frustrating years on a dozen quickly forgotten musicals. When he finished the libretto and lyrics for the thirteenth, he gave them to his new collaborator, Richard Rodgers. They called it *Oklahoma!* and it ran for five years and 2,212 performances in the US alone. It was just as successful in England where revivals still regularly break box office records.

I had to wait two years before I was able to see the show. It was wartime and I was serving in the navy in the South Pacific. But Dad did write me about the success of the premiere. Considering how reserved he was in speech and praise, the letter is one of my treasured possessions. In the final paragraph he wrote, 'We're all happy and well, especially me, I guess. My only speck of cloud is that I miss your not being here to share this. But in a quite conventional and old-fashioned way I am very proud that you are where you are and doing what you are doing. Love, Dad.'

My father was a striking figure. Standing over six feet tall, with a crew cut and intense blue eyes, he was a calm presence amid the routine hysteria of the theatre world. He was baptised Oscar Greeley Clendenning Hammerstein II, Dad's mother and her family, the Nimmos, were Episcopalian; his father's people were German Jews. Dad was profoundly devoted to his mother, and her death, when he was twelve, affected him deeply. He taught me to treat my own mother, my sister, Alice, and all women with courtesy and respect. In his work he created strong, dignified, beloved female characters – Mother Superior in *The Sound of Music,* Cousin Nettie in *Carousel,* and Aunt Eller in *Oklahoma!* To an extent they were all tributes to my grandmother.

Dad's father, though, was not enthusiastic about Dad's being involved in the theatre. Before dying, my grandfather extracted a promise from his brother Arthur, a Broadway producer, to 'never let Oscar near a stage'. He wanted his son to have a proper education and profession. Dad dutifully attended Columbia Law School in New York. But he also collaborated on three campus productions, even giving himself a fat part in one. Then, after a year in a Manhattan law office, Dad pleaded with Uncle Arthur to let him go to work for him. 'I belong in the theatre!' he insisted. Finally Uncle Arthur relented and gave Dad a £10-a-week job as an assistant stage-manager.

Uncle Arthur thought his idealistic young nephew would soon be disillusioned by the long, thankless hours and scant pay. But Dad immersed himself in the backstage toil of mounting a show. There he learned stagecraft and developed the discipline that would keep him working through the lean years following *Show Boat* and his Hollywood stint.

Above all, Dad was a hard worker. Many of his lyrics were poems destined to be married to music. But there were times when he would spend days searching for the exact word to express the reality of our laughter, tears, hopes and dreams. Richard Rodgers said, 'Oscar's a dreamer, but a very careful dreamer.'

Throughout the lyrics of the more than 1,000 songs Dad wrote run themes of optimism and hope, and the idea that the impossible is always possible. Perhaps that's why one critic termed songs like 'You'll Never Walk Alone' from *Carousel* 'secular hymns'. In *South Pacific* Mary Martin sang 'A Cock-eyed Optimist', an anthem to hope. And how many high school graduates, poised on the threshold of adulthood, have adopted 'Climb Ev'ry Mountain' from *The Sound of Music* as their class song?

I remember a story Dad used to tell about a vacation he took in Guatemala. He'd climbed to the top of a towering, thousand-year-old Mayan pyramid. It seemed as if he had only to reach out his hand to touch the sun-gilded edge of the clouds above. But when he looked back down at the dizzyingly steep descent, Dad froze. He was sure he would slip and fall. He was trapped at the top of the pyramid. What did he do? 'So I climbed down,' he said. 'When you find yourself in a trap that you can't get out of by any other way except what looks to be impossible, you do what you think is impossible.'

It was his infectious optimism that made my father so attractive. 'To a person who's never seen a tree,' he once said, 'you wouldn't describe it only as it looks in winter.' At Christmas time our home was filled with relatives, friends and Dad's classmates going all the way back to grammar school. 'Oscar never lost a friend,' an old schoolmate once declared.

For Dad, loving others was the perfect way to love God. 'We belong to one another,' he said. 'The oneness on earth is the same as our oneness with God.' Dad despised prejudice and persecution. He thought bigoted people had been taught to hate. He even wrote a song about it, 'You've Got to Be Carefully Taught'. What audiences sensed in Dad's lyrics, I believe, was his essential decency. Without that quality he could never have written lyrics that still inspire people all over the world.

One morning Dad was late for rehearsal for a version of *Cinderella* he and Rodgers had written for television. Hurrying to the studio, Dad impatiently bolted off the kerb, ignoring the Don't Walk sign. A policeman shouted and motioned him back. Dad was annoyed with himself; now he would be even later for rehearsal while the officer wrote him a well-deserved jaywalking ticket.

But the tough New York City cop surprised him by asking, 'Aren't you Oscar Hammerstein?' When Dad nodded, the policeman said, 'I just wanted to tell you how my wife and I and our kids love your songs.'

Dad thanked him somewhat sheepishly and started to hurry off, but the officer stopped him with, 'Say, do you mind if I ask you a question? Are you religious?'

Dad paused. But before he could reply, the policeman answered his own question. 'Ah, you're a religious guy, all right. I can tell by the kind of songs you write!'

What that policeman had discovered in Dad's work was my father's underlying faith. Faith in mankind, faith in something greater and more powerful than mankind, and faith that good can triumph over evil.

For my father, faith was always more of a verb than a noun.

RUBY

by Hayes Beachum

A story of one man and his dog.

I didn't feel much like having a party, but up at the house they were getting ready for my eightieth birthday. I stood gloomily in the yard watching my son, Wayne, play with the dog, the only one left from the English-shepherd business I'd let fade out two years earlier.

In my honour, Wayne and his wife, Geneva, my two daughters and their husbands, all the grandchildren and even some of my brothers and sisters had gathered. But why celebrate? What was the point of their spending time with a dismal old stick-in-the-mud like me?

Wayne gave the dog a final pat and turned to me. 'Why not breed her again, Dad?'

I started fussing with the latch on the dog pound. 'It's a shame not to,' I said, 'but ever since Ruby disappeared I don't have it in me to raise a litter of pups.' And that was the truth of it.

Wayne's arm slid across my shoulders. 'I understand, Dad. The whole family loved that dog ...' His voice trailed off and he changed the subject. 'Let's get up to the house. Must be close to party time.'

I trudged along with Wayne, trying to swallow the lump that still rose up in my throat every time I thought of Ruby. She'd come into my life after I'd sold my petrol station and retired. Well, not exactly retired.

'I refuse to just sit in that rocking chair on the porch,' I'd told my wife, Estelle.

After fifty years of being married to me, she knew I needed to be busy with something, and she'd nodded. 'You'll come up with something. Always have.'

After a while, in one of the farm magazines, I came across an article on English shepherds. It explained what good working dogs they are and how you could start a profitable part-time business with them. So I'd bought a couple of dogs, and before long people were waiting in line to buy the puppies as soon as they were weaned.

It was productive work, paid fairly well and kept me busy. But I was careful not to become personally attached to the dogs. I hadn't had time for a dog of my own before and it was too late in life to 'have' a dog now. That was for young boys. So mainly the puppies came and went. I took good care of them, fed them well and exercised them, but that was all.

Until Ruby. I knew from the moment I saw that pup that there was something different about her. It wasn't just the soft puppy fur that hinted of a shiny sable coat to come, or the snowy white bib and collar. It wasn't her gentle, loveable nature. All the other dogs had those same features. No, there was something special about her eyes, a searching gaze that reached clear through the all-business attitude I'd kept with the other dogs.

Ruby grew quickly, and before I knew it, she was begging to be let outside. But instead of scampering across the garden like the rest of the youngsters, she stuck at my heels, following me as I did the chores. It wasn't long until she started jumping up onto the seat beside me in my old truck and riding out to the old family farm, where I still kept a few cattle. She'd help round them up, then sit down beside me while we watched them munch the hay we'd brought.

The day I'd had my heart attack out there at the farm, she'd stayed right by my side, licking my face and whining me back to consciousness. I had finally managed to get a grip on her collar, and together we'd made it back to the truck. She sat close beside me in her usual seat as we crawled back home in low gear.

After that she was as much a part of me as my right arm. As she got older I taught her a few special tricks. I'd hold out a stick and she'd jump over it, or I'd form a circle with my arms and she'd jump through. But it was her own idea to go ahead of me into the fields and flush out snakes. How long had she done that? Nine or ten years, as long as I'd had her. Or maybe it'd be better to say 'as long as she'd had me'.

That day I came home from church and found her gone, I thought I'd just forgotten to close the gate and she'd surely show up by supper. But she didn't come back. I spent days, weeks, driving up and down back roads and highways, looking for any sign of her. I advertised on the radio and in the newspapers. But nothing helped. She was gone.

'Don't give up,' Estelle kept telling me. 'Where's your faith anyway?'

Where indeed? The fact of the matter is, I was losing it. And a lot of other things changed after that. I didn't have the gumption to raise dogs anymore. Days that had once been spent following Ruby across the fields seemed to drag. I tried to summon up the drive that had carried me through some mighty tough years, but it seemed to be gone. So I began to feel sorry for myself and stray far from the God I'd always trusted.

At the house everybody acted excited about my birthday, but I couldn't help but ask myself why they were all here. I knew the youngsters would rather be with their friends. And if my son and daughters would admit it, there were probably other things they'd prefer doing. After all, I was just someone they had to come and visit, someone not much good to anyone anymore.

We got through lunch, then went outside to cut the cake Estelle had baked. I made an effort to act like always, declaring that the grandchildren would have to help me blow out the candles and joking about how there was enough fire there to keep warm during a blizzard. Later I sat out on the porch in that rocking chair I swore I'd never use, faking a nap, while my grandson, Charles, played with his cars and the ladyfolk searched the flower beds for early bloomers.

Gradually I found myself watching my granddaughters, Shearra and Beth, as they tried to shoo away an old stray dog, coat dusty and matted, that kept wandering into the yard. As I watched, Estelle joined them. The harder they tried to scare off the dog, the more determined it was to stay. Just when they'd think it was gone, the mutt would reappear, sneaking under the bushes or around the back of the house.

'Come on,' I heard Wayne say to Geneva, 'let's go help Grandma and the girls.'

The five of them played hide-and-seek with the old dog for a while, then quite suddenly Wayne and Geneva stopped chasing and stood off to the side talking. Before I knew it, the whole family seemed to be whispering.

'What's the matter with them anyway?' I asked myself, and I got up for a better look.

They were all staring at that stray dog. The poor animal was in even worse shape than I had thought at first. Its hair was coming out in patches, and the coat looked like one giant brillo pad. The old fella must have been out in the fields for months.

'Dad,' Wayne spoke softly. 'Dad, come on over here.' Geneva picked up a stick and held it out a foot or two from the ground. The stray saw it, moved towards it, studied it for a moment, then sat down before it.

I moved closer. A twig snapped under my boot, and the dog turned and stared up at me. Its eyes were soft, velvet, and its gaze … its gaze … it was a searching gaze that went right through to the heart of me. The dog turned and, moving as if in slow motion, jumped smoothly over the stick.

My control was beginning to crumble. I was almost scared to hope. Yet I had to know for sure. I formed my arms into a circle and waited, afraid even to look.

But a nudge against my leg forced me to look into the velvet eyes again. Then with what seemed barely an effort, Ruby leapt through the circle, her matted fur grazing my arms.

All at once everyone was shouting and crying and hugging. There was no doubt! Ruby had come back!

I dropped down beside Ruby on the grass and pulled her onto my lap. 'Whoever stole her must have taken her a long way away,' Wayne exclaimed. 'Wonder how far she travelled.' I took a rough paw in my hand and examined the worn pad, marvelling at the courage it must have taken her to get back home, the determination, the persistence.

The thought then came streaking into my head: Ruby hadn't given up. But I had. I had given up on life. On the blessings that were all around me. Even on the faith that told me clearly to keep on and not be faint.

'What's happened to this party?' I shouted. 'Let's keep this party going. After all, it isn't every day a man celebrates his eightieth birthday!'

I got to my feet and slipped my arms around Beth and Shearra as we walked back towards the house with Ruby twining in and out of our legs.

NOT SO DIFFERENT

by Caroline Rubino

What is it like to live your whole life with a severe facial deformity? Here is one woman who knows.

I work as a nurse at a New York hospital, helping care for sick and premature infants in intensive care. When I gaze down at those tiny bundles tethered to IV equipment as they struggle to hang on to life, I am moved. Those special babies seem to reach deep down inside for something extra, something that's there for all of us when we really need it. Sometimes I lean over and assure them that all of their struggling is worth it. Life is worth it.

I've had to fight hard in my own life. To look at me, you might wonder why I try. I have a facial disfigurement, the result of a genetic condition doctors call 'NF' – neurofibromatosis. It was formerly known as Elephant Man's Disease, after John Merrick, the turn-of-the-century England's famous 'Elephant Man'. Merrick's facial disfigurement relegated him to carnival freak shows, caged like an animal or chained up for the public to gasp at. Maybe you've heard of the play or film *The Elephant Man*. They're about Merrick, and how a compassionate, enlightened doctor rescued him. We've come a way since then, but people still gape at the facially disfigured. Some still see us as grotesque.

And doctors still rescue us. Modern surgery has made enormous strides. I'm a case in point. The benign tumours associated with my form of NF make my face lumpy and misshapen. I've had more than a dozen reconstructive procedures in my thirty-three years, starting in childhood. In fact, surgery was as much a part of my growing up as a skipping rope or hop-scotch. I had X-rays the way some kids have snapshots taken for the family album. Summertime, when other kids were playing and swimming and going off to camp, I was facing surgery. We planned it that way so I wouldn't miss much school.

My first major operation was at age four, another at six, then more. There was always something the surgeons thought they could do for me, and I was always willing for them to try. Still, I can't forget hearing a doctor tell my parents, 'We can help Caroline's appearance up to a point. But she'll never be a hundred percent.'

A hundred percent. That phrase haunted me. A hundred percent what? My heart, my mind, my character – they weren't deformed. I was a complete person, not a reject. I just looked different. I decided from that point on that in everything I tried I would give one hundred percent. I would act as if I was a hundred percent, no matter what.

I grew up in a little neighbourhood, full of decent, working-class families. We were a community. I had the same neighbours, the same friends and the same classmates from nursery school to college. They got used to the way I looked. Still, there were times when kids who didn't know me would run away from me on the street. Once, a new mother in the neighbourhood refused to let her daughters play with me. In primary school a classmate shouted, 'What happened, did you blow a bubble the wrong way?' I just couldn't help it – I ran out of school and all the way home, in tears. Even so, I truly believed what the nuns at St Francis school taught me: God loves each and every one of His creations. I felt God's love.

And I felt the love of my parents. I remember the hours spent with my mother as I sat before a mirror while she brushed my hair – my thick, beautiful dark hair – and we talked. 'Mummy,' I'd ask, 'why am I like this?'

'I don't know, Caroline,' she'd say tenderly, 'but it's okay, dear. You are a child of God. You are made in His image, and you are loved. It's okay.'

And it was okay.

After cosy little St Francis, St Nicholas High School was huge, terrifying. Secondary school, remember, is when kids suddenly get obsessed with looking good. Now it felt as if everyone was looking at me, and I'd scuttle into classrooms, eyes glued to the floor, wishing I was invisible. One day in that first year, I stopped in the girls' toilets between classes. There stood a gaggle of my new classmates, craning their necks at the big mirror over the sinks.

'I simply can't go to that dance Friday with this big zit on my chin!' exploded one, verging on hysteria. 'What am I going to do?'

She and her girlfriends barely noticed me standing there, down at one end of the long row of sinks. When the bell rang they put away their makeup and rushed off to class.

I stood staring at myself. That girl didn't know what it was really like to look different. All she had to worry about was a pimple. Pimples can be covered up and will go away, but I couldn't cover up my face.

And then it struck me. Maybe that pimple had caused her as much anguish as my NF sometimes caused me. For that instant beneath the unforgiving glare of those fluorescent lights, she and I shared the same anxiety about ourselves. And oddly enough, I felt as though I belonged. I was not so different from other people after all.

Beauty's only skin deep, the old saying goes. Well, that's true for those who look different too. Once other kids at St Nicholas got past the surface, once they got to know me for who I was inside, they almost invariably liked me. They really liked me! Slowly, tentatively, I started making friends outside.

Eventually I went to college. I trained as an occupational therapist, and then the time came when I knew I had to leave home and stand on my own two feet. I needed to get out in the world.

The move was more traumatic than I'd figured, not so much for me as for my mum and dad. They'd always tried so hard to protect me – to overprotect me. I sometimes felt they were always afraid of seeing me get hurt. I was moving only a few blocks away to a basement apartment in my sister's house, but you would have thought I was leaving the country.

When the day came, the suitcases were stacked neatly in our front hall, and my brother and brother-in-law loaded the van. Mum stood off to one side. Dad paced and stared at the floor, arms tightly folded. I took a deep breath and a last look around at the house where I had spent my whole life. Mum's eyes brimmed. Dad stopped pacing. And as I looked at them, I realised how much I loved them for bringing me into this world, how blessed I really was. I thought back to when Mum would soothe me by running a brush through my hair. I remembered her telling me how much she and Dad loved me and how everything would be okay. I wrapped my arms around her.

'It's okay, Mum,' I whispered. 'It's okay.'

That was ten years ago. Today I live in a flat I bought myself. I went back to college to get a nursing degree. I continue to have reconstructive surgeries. One benefit of a procedure I recently had was that my mouth became straighter. Now I can smile. I always wanted a real smile.

And like anyone else, I want to look good. I pay attention to my wardrobe. I put on make-up when I go out, not to hide anything but to enhance. I want to look my best, to look a hundred percent.

I identify with those babies I help in intensive care, and with the way they fight for life. Helping them helps me understand that life is worth living.

I still get stares – most of us with disfigurements do – but I can live with that. You see, I know that in God's eyes I'm beautiful, because, as someone once said to me, the Lord doesn't look at the outside, but on the inside.

A DESPERATE RACE

by Mary Jane Chambers

A woman driving alone at night and a stalking car.

I opened the pages of the newspaper and stared. A gang of robber-rapists, the paper reported, were prowling the streets preying on women driving alone at night. The armed thugs would follow their victim on a lonely stretch of road, harassing her until she pulled over and stopped. Dozens of women had been victimised in the past month.

I looked at the story for a long time – but I already knew certain details all too well. My thoughts flashed back to the night two weeks before when I too drove alone on a five-mile stretch of the road described. I had attended a committee meeting until about 9.10 p.m. When I got into my car to go home, out of habit I locked the doors. I was not especially concerned about driving home alone. After all, I'd been married for thirty years and had two grown sons. I had led a protected life, really. Nobody had ever tried to harm me.

I drove two streets down Belleview Avenue and swung into the car park. My husband and I often drove this way on Sunday mornings, when there were picnickers along the roadside and boaters on the canal. But now the recreation areas that bordered the road were deserted; there were no streetlights, and in the dark, the Park so busy during the day, seemed desolate. I wish I hadn't come this way, I thought.

Traffic was light. There were only a few cars in sight, all behind me. I stayed in the right lane while three of them passed me and sped off into the night. A fourth car pulled up behind me. And stayed there. Apparently its driver was content to follow along at my speed. But the car did seem to be unusually close. I glanced in my rear-view mirror, wondering if the driver realised how close he was to me. I guessed he didn't.

Then the car drew even closer. Suddenly their headlights flashed their bright beams. I gasped in surprise, quickly tilting up the mirror so I wouldn't be blinded by the glare. But their lights still lit up the interior of my car. Did they have some kind of spotlight?

Now I was worried. I had the strange feeling they were watching me intently. Why were they doing this? Were they kids out on a joyride? Whoever they were, this was a bad joke. And dangerous. 'Dear God,' I prayed, 'make them pass me.'

But if anything, they came closer. Bolder and bolder, they were now inches from my back bumper, their lights still trained on my head.

We went a mile, then two. They could see me clearly – but I couldn't see them. It seemed to me I'd seen two people in the front seat and another in the back. I wasn't sure. But now it was chillingly clear that these weren't just kids out on a lark. Whoever the dark figures in that car were, they were stalking me. I felt defenceless and alone.

Near panic, I held tight to the steering wheel as though it could somehow take me out of this danger.

'Please, God,' I prayed, 'help me to know what to do.'

Even before I finished speaking, I felt calmer. I unclenched my fingers and held the steering wheel more lightly. My shoulders relaxed, then my thoughts. And as my panic lessened, a voice sounded firmly in my mind.

Keep going. Don't stop.

But I couldn't stand those lights another minute. If I pulled over, they'd just pass me – wouldn't they? And the ordeal would be over.

You're on a four-lane roadway that is practically deserted. They could pass you if they wanted to. Keep moving.

Like a student reviewing a problem in arithmetic, I thought of possible things I could do. I thought about turning off down one of the side roads. Again the inner voice:

You don't know this area very well. You could get lost or cornered.

I passed a sign that read, 'Speed Limit 40, Police Cameras'.

If I speed up, I thought, I may be able to attract the attention of the police. This time the inner voice was silent. I pressed my foot on the accelerator and saw the speedometer zoom to 75 miles an hour.

For a few seconds I was free of the other car, but soon it was back at my bumper again. And no police car – or any car – appeared.

I went faster still, pulled ahead a bit, then slowed. So did they. The slower speed was even worse – torture in slow motion.

The feeling of fear took over again. My knuckles were white on the steering wheel. Again I was on the verge of stopping.

Is there something wrong with your car? said the inner voice.

I would have laughed if I hadn't been so frightened. My husband, a car fancier, faithfully kept our car running well.

Are you low on gas?

No, my husband just filled the tank.

Do you have a flat tyre?

Obviously not.

This checklist cleared my head. I had no real reason to stop – and if I did I'd be putting myself in the hands of these strangers. I drove on.

Suddenly, to my own surprise, I began to sing. 'Amazing Grace' and other hymns. My pursuers were flooding my car with glaring light, and I sang as loudly as I could.

I was still trembling. But I was determined not to surrender. I began to think of how I could outwit my pursuers.

And you will think of something, the inner voice said. God is with you.

I was in familiar territory now, approaching the turnoff that would take me to my neighbourhood. As the intersection appeared,

I pretended I was going to stop at the stop sign. At the last possible moment, I turned the wheel and stepped on the accelerator instead. My car careered around the corner, tyres screeching. I raced down the highway like an Indianapolis Speedway driver.

My pursuers were thrown off – but only for a moment. They seemed to be fumbling with their gears, and by the time they recovered, I was almost a street ahead. Out of the reach of their glaring lights.

Again the inner voice spoke before fear could take hold. Keep moving, it said. Don't stop. God is with you.

Before my pursuers could catch up with me, again, another car entered from a side street, inserting itself between us.

I turned off the highway onto Maryland Avenue, heading for home. In my rear-view mirror I saw my pursuers turn too. But the other car had slowed them down and given me the lead I needed.

The road curved abruptly to the right – and there, momentarily concealed by the bend, was the entrance to my street! I swerved left again and raced towards my house. When I was barely a block away, I saw my tormentors shoot past behind me, pursuing me in the wrong direction. From the way they were speeding, they would be blocks away before realising they had lost me.

After following me down three different roads, they had missed the last turn! As I shut and locked the door of my car behind me, I almost cried with relief. My house is in a cul-de-sac. If they hadn't missed that last turn they might have trapped me.

Now, two weeks later, as I looked at the newspaper account about these criminals, I felt horror – and yet a feeling of strength as well. 'Aren't you terrified to go out at night now?' a friend had asked when I told her my story.

I'm definitely more cautious now. I always take sensible precautions when driving alone, especially after dark. But I'm not cowering in my house, living the life of a timid recluse. Fear didn't cause me to panic and pull over that night, and it's not going to stop me now. I may drive down another dark road where terror and desperation await. Or I may find myself faced with some other emergency that seems hopeless.

I know now that my hope and security resides in God, who guides me down every road and through every crisis. Whatever comes, I will never have to face it alone.

IN RESERVE

by Pamela Gordon

Young love inspires faith.

In remote parts of the Alps, I have been told, mountaineers leave caches of food at strategic places along difficult trails so that other climbers can use them when caught in a blizzard or facing other dangers. I believe God plants certain scenes in our memories today, from which we can draw strength or encouragement when needed.

One day in our town quite a few years ago my husband and I stopped our car at a red traffic light. Walking along the sidewalk was a young sailor with white Navy cap and bell-bottom trousers, carrying a seabag on his shoulder. He came to a modest house and bounded up the porch steps. As he did, the door was flung open and a young woman rushed out, hair flying, arms outstretched, a smile of radiant happiness on her face. The sailor dropped his seabag and caught her in his arms. They clung together with such intensity that you knew he had been gone for a long time. But now he was home, safe, and the joy that radiated from that couple lit up the steps, the street, the whole world.

My husband and I looked at each other. How wonderful! our glances said. Then the light changed and we moved on. But to this day, whenever I pass that spot I feel the warmth and the gladness – and the miracle – of young love, and something in me is restored and strengthened.

THE LOST FAMILY

by Jacqueline Lasky

A Polish father finds his hidden treasure.

I recently experienced a heart-warming union that had an effect on me that will last me the rest of my life. I accompanied my father on a journey back to Poland. Before World War II, my father escaped from his little town in Poland and went to America. Being Jewish, my father was fortunate to escape Hitler and was privileged to fight for the Allies during the war. Content with his life as an American citizen, my father never returned to Poland. He said he never felt a need to see his mother country again. Until recently. One summer, my father was drawn back to Poland.

I had mixed emotions about being in Poland. This was my country, my culture, and I felt an anticipated sensation. At the same time, the Polish government was still communist then, and the people had an extensive history of anti-Semitism. But I still felt the energy of being there. We rented a car and hired a driver and began our journey in search of the small village of Krynki, near the Russian border. My father did not hope to find some long lost relative. There were no Jews left in Krynki after the Nazi occupation during World War II. We drove around, not knowing where to go. My father instructed the driver to stop the car on the side of a bridge. We all got out and looked around. After a couple of minutes we saw a woman about my father's age. She spoke no English, my father spoke no Polish, but there was a common small knowledge of German. Breaking through the barriers, we were able to communicate. I could feel a special bond between us.

We told her our story. Her face brightened and she stopped her yard work. She called her husband in from the field and invited us into their home. It was a small house but very comfortable. From their appearance it was obvious this couple had worked hard all their lives. With what little they had, they welcomed us as long lost family. We ate and drank, and I felt like I belonged there. This couple had lived in Krynki all their lives. They saw the destruction created by World War II. They had tried their best to survive. I could feel the bond between us strengthen.

Then they brought something down from the top of a shelf. It was wrapped up in brown tissue paper and seemed not to have been touched in years. It was a parchment piece of a Torah scroll. After the war, the couple had been digging in the ruins of the Jewish ghetto. After they discovered the scroll, they wrapped it up and put it in safekeeping. This big-hearted couple knew someone would someday come for it. They eagerly gave the scroll to us to take home. Tears came to my father's eyes. My father and I were the people intended to have the Torah scroll.

The portion of the Torah on the parchment described the distribution of the people of Israel into the tribes of the sons of Jacob. It says the people will survive, through the good and bad times, and will prove themselves righteous and worthy. On that summer day, I understood its meaning. We had met benevolent people who unselfishly gave to us something as precious as life. This hardworking, honest couple lived a modest life with a strong following of their Catholic faith. Although we were separated by thousands of miles, we were meant to meet someday in a meaningful union. It is hard to realise that strangers make such a big impact on a person's life. Everyone is affected by one another, and the actions of each person affect the whole world. Was it 'fate' that made my father stop on that particular street? I still feel a tingling sensation when I see the Torah scroll hanging on our wall. My goal in life is to be like that loving couple. I want to develop the characteristics of being kind, gentle, unselfish, hardworking, honest and motivated. I am guided by the faith that there is good in all men. When the goodwill of all men emerges, there will be peace across the world. It begins with just one person at a time.

THE LAST WILL

by Don Tullis

Those precious last words.

Some time ago a disastrous mine tragedy, killing many, occurred in West Virginia. One of the miners was a man named Josh Chafins. Somewhere in his dark, damp prison, when all hope of release had gone, he had found a bit of ragged paper and had written upon it his word of farewell to his wife:

'I love you more than you can ever know, take care of the kids and raise them to serve God.'

Josh Chafins left neither gold nor valuable property but probably the richest possessions in all the world – love and faith.

THE WAYWARD ARROW

by Beau Bridges

An actor from a family of actors recalls his first mysterious encounter with faith.

When was the first time you became aware of God? For me, it happened in an odd way when I was a kid. It was the summer when archery was the craze among my friends. And, of all things, it was an arrow that first led me to think about God.

I was a boy, just twelve, growing up. My father, Lloyd Bridges, was a film actor, and my brother, Jeff, my sister, Lucinda, and I did the same kinds of things other kids did – like mowing lawns for extra money. We had chores around the house, and we loved hanging out with friends.

In fact, I was hanging out with a bunch of my pals the day this strange thing happened. We had brought our bows and arrows to a field about two miles from my house. We had made our own arrows that summer, gluing coloured feathers to the ends and painting the shafts so that each was unique. That day I was using my favourite arrow; it had red dots outlined in black, and I'd stuck black and red feathers on the end. There was, I felt, no swifter arrow in my collection.

We weren't using targets. Instead we were playing a game we'd created on our own, one of those crazy, 'death-defying' games that boys that age seem to love. We had played this game many times that summer, and the fact that it was dangerous only heightened the excitement.

We would stand in a tight-knit group in the middle of the field. Each of us would put an arrow on his bowstring, then pull it back and raise the bow so that the arrow was pointing up, perpendicular to the ground. Then someone would call out 'Let 'em fly', and we would all shoot our arrows at once.

The arrows would zoom up into the sky, out of sight. Then we'd listen for their return. We knew that, having flown straight up, they would be falling straight down, and we huddled in morbid anticipation, hoping they wouldn't be hitting us. The object of the game was to have the arrows land as close to the group as possible without, of course, hurting anyone. The winner was the owner of the arrow that hit the nearest.

That day when I heard the call 'Let 'em fly' my bowstring reverberated with a loud zing and I watched the polka-dotted shaft of my favourite arrow whiz up into the sun's rays and disappear. Soon we heard zump, zump, zump, and the arrows began falling all around us. When they stopped, everyone rushed to claim his, and several of the guys shouted, 'Mine is the closest!' I looked around, but mine was missing. It was strange. My arrow should have landed close to the others, but there was no trace of it.

I covered every inch of the field, and my friend helped, but we couldn't find it. Doggedly, I continued. I was disappointed, and felt a little silly and puzzled. Where was it? Mine went up with the rest. It should come down with the rest. It made me feel, well, kind of eerie.

Earlier I had promised to help my mate mow a neighbour's lawn. Chuck was ready to go to our job, but I wanted to search some more.

'Come on,' he yelled at me, 'it's time to go.'

'Let's look just a few more minutes,' I begged. 'It's bound to be here.'

'Look,' said Chuck, 'you promised to help me this afternoon. Now, c'mon, we've got to go!'

It's funny how something as small as an arrow can mean so much to you when you're twelve. But I felt strangely sad, as though

I'd lost a kind of friend. A lot of myself had gone into making it. I had shown it to my father and friends, and everyone had complimented me and made a big deal over it.

And now it was gone. Probably buried in the matted grass. I visualised it snapping under the weight of someone's foot, and groaned. And now I had to go and help Chuck; I couldn't back out of that. I had promised.

Have you ever wished very hard for something, with all your energy, even though you knew it would be incredible if it ever really happened? Well, that's how it was with me and that arrow. While I was helping Chuck cut grass, I daydreamed about finding it.

When we finished our work, I waved goodbye to Chuck and headed home. Then, for some reason I can't explain, I was suddenly bursting with energy. I felt good! I wanted to run. And did I! I raced at top speed down the street. I charged along not knowing the reason for my elation, and then, out of breath, I slowed down to a walk. Ahead of me was a great tree whose branches reached out across the pathway. My clothes were sticking to my sweaty body, and my breath was coming in great gasps; the tree offered welcome shade from the sun, and as I drew nearer, I lifted my head up slightly and felt grateful for the coolness.

My eyes rested for a moment on the tree's gnarled branches; the leaves fluttered. Something red and black fluttered too. I glanced down along the trunk and over to the other side of the tree, but the bit of red and black pulled my eyes back. A bird? ... No ... My brain did a double take, and I came to a startled halt. I blinked. Yes! There it was! My arrow! Two miles from where I had shot it!

I felt happy and bewildered all at once. The question – How did it get there? – kept turning in my mind. Could it have been carried along on a wind current, then dropped down into the tree? That seemed unlikely. And why this tree, along this path? Could some kids have found it and thrown it up into the branches? Still, no one – not even I – knew I'd be coming down this path; there were other ways home. Why did I choose this one? How did I happen to look up just in time to see the black and red feathers?

I was stumped. The arrow couldn't have travelled two miles on the power I had used in drawing back on the bowstring when I let it fly. I knew I wasn't that strong.

'Wow,' I said out loud. I reached up to grab the arrow. Something super human, super strong. Something so immense that I couldn't understand how it was involved here. It made me feel a little weird, a little scared. As I took my arrow in hand again, a shiver ran down my spine.

That was the moment when I had my very first intimation of God.

It was a little thing, my finding that arrow, but it was something that had happened to me – it was my own special mystery. For the first time in my life I had to accept something I couldn't understand, and I was in awe of it.

From that day on I began attending church and Sunday school with new interest, learning about faith, talking to God, praying the Lord's Prayer – which became a part of my daily life. As I grew older, I discovered that my experience with the arrow that summer's day was but a tiny sample of what religion is all about. Faith in God is a mixture of mystery and awe. You cannot see it or touch it; it requires only that we accept and believe.

And that has been my understanding of faith ever since. It is something that I like to talk about to my own sons, Casey, twelve, and Jordan, eight. Casey is just the age I was when I shot my red-and-black arrow into the sky. Yet I wonder if he can really comprehend my story. I wonder if faith doesn't come to everyone differently, in some mysterious way.

THE SILKEN THREAD

by Nien Cheng

During China's cultural revolution this diminutive woman was able to endure six-and-a-half years of brutal imprisonment, humiliation and torture.

In September 1966, after the outbreak of the Cultural Revolution in China and the destruction of my home by the Red Guards, I was taken to a 'struggle meeting' where I was physically abused for four hours. Then I was thrown into a dank, dirty cell of the No. 1 Detention House, the dreaded prison for political suspects in Shanghai.

Over my head hung a single naked light bulb, under my feet the floor was black with dampness. Cobwebs hung in thick ropes from the ceiling, the walls were crusted with grime. My bed was bare rough planks, my toilet was a crude concrete cube in one corner of the cell. The air was heavy. I stretched up and pulled with all my strength at the cell's only small window, high up in the wall. It swung open in a shower of dirt and paint chips to reveal rusty iron bars.

For many weeks before they broke into my home, Mao Zedong's fanatical Red Guards had roamed the streets of Shanghai, ransacking homes and brutalising citizens suspected of 'Western' sympathies. Since both my late husband and I had worked for Shell International Petroleum Company, I fell under that category.

On the night of 30 August, the Red Guards, nearly forty of them, burst into my home to 'take revolutionary action' and destroy the Four Olds: old culture, old customs, old habits and old ways of thinking. They shredded clothes and upholstery, smashed dishes and mirrors, threw the books into a bonfire on the lawn and confiscated my valuables.

At least my twenty-three-year-old daughter, Meiping, was at work when they burst in. She was the dearest person in the world to me. Intelligent, beautiful and warm-hearted, she was an actress at the Shanghai Film Studio. But what would become of her now that I had been denounced and imprisoned as a 'running dog of the Western imperialists'?

Never in my life had I been so alone. I sank down on my 'bed' in despair, closed my eyes and asked God for His guidance. My husband had come from one of China's earliest Christian families and I had spent many hours with his mother, reading the Bible to her when her eyesight was failing. I had become a Christian myself, and so far my faith had carried me through many trying circumstances. God would not fail me now.

That moment of prayer strengthened my resolve. I went to the cell door and pounded as hard as I could.

The small shutter on the door slid open and a guard's face appeared.

'What do you want?'

'Please give me a broom to sweep this room,' I said. 'It's very dirty.'

The guard was clearly startled at my request. 'Nonsense!' she said angrily. The shutter closed again with a smack.

In the past I had found that taking positive action to cope with problems was therapeutic and good for the renewal of courage. To make my dreary quarters more liveable was now my challenge. I pulled the bed out and, using my meagre ration of rough toilet paper, did my best to wipe the grime from it. Little good it did, but the effort made me feel better. With the light bulb still glaring above me, I fell into a fitful sleep.

Towards morning, the light was finally switched off. The shutter in the door opened again, and an aluminium container holding some watery rice porridge and a few pickled vegetables was thrust into my hands.

As I quietly said my morning prayers, I heard the door shutter slide open. 'What are you doing?' a voice beyond the door cried out harshly. 'You must read Chairman Mao's books!'

But once more my moment of prayer had revived my fighting spirit and I asked her again for a broom to clean the cell.

To my surprise, she squeezed an old ragged broom through the opening above the door. I pulled my bed around the cell and stood on it, using the broom as a brush to pull down the cobwebs. I sighed in relief – that was a victory.

I went to my cell door again and called out. When the guard came, I recited a quotation from Mao: 'To be hygienic is glorious; to be unhygienic is a shame.' Then I quickly asked, 'May I have some water to clean my cell?'

I used the water to wipe my bed and the panes of the window. Then I bathed myself and rinsed out my blouse. With some rice I'd saved from my midday meal, I made a paste and glued toilet paper along the wall by the bed to make a clean wall surface beside it.

Sitting on my bed, I looked at the narrow strip of sky just visible through the window bars. That day and the next I watched a rectangular patch of sunlight move across my cell floor. Then the days moved into weeks and the weeks into months.

I was constantly hungry and exhausted, and my health deteriorated. The isolation was broken only by periods of intense, brutal and irrational interrogation about 'crimes' I had never committed. Since I could not pray openly, I had to do so while my head was bent over Mao's *Little Red Book* that I was told to read for my 're-education'.

And my daughter, Meiping? I worried about her constantly. Was she safe? I did not know. I was isolated from the world outside, and the world of my cell grew lonelier and lonelier until …

One day when I was staring up at the window, I saw a spider about the size of a pea, making its slow but steady way up one of the rust-encrusted bars.

The spider moved purposefully to the top of the window and then, after a moment's pause, swung out and down on a slender thread that emerged as if by magic from its own tiny body. Working with precision, it attached the end of the silken thread to a lower bar, then made its way back up the thread to where it had started, and swung out again to anchor another thread on another bar.

I sat motionless, almost holding my breath, as the tiny spider moved methodically from corner to corner, until what looked like a frame had been created. Then it made its way within that frame, from corner to corner, edge to edge, creating a pattern that was evenly spaced and intricately beautiful.

At last the web was completed. The spider waited in its lacy centre.

By the time the spider had finished its work, it was early evening. Golden light streamed through the cell's small window. The rays of the setting sun struck the web and turned it into a glittering mass of rainbow colours.

I sat in stunned silence. In this ugly cell, before my eyes, beauty had come into being. The spider, one of the tiniest of God's creatures, had made me feel a part of God's world again. It was a moment of transcendence.

In the first light of day I looked to see if the spider was still there. It was. 'Good morning,' I murmured, and that was the beginning of our friendship. Every morning when I first opened my eyes, I looked for the spider and greeted it. And at night I looked over as I went to sleep, reassured by its steady presence.

Day by day, my affection for the spider grew. If a corner of its web was ruffled by a breeze or ripped by the wind, the spider was there in an instant to repair the damage. Again and again it patched and weaved and restored, never retreating from the wind or giving in to defeat.

With each passing day, the temperature dropped. Winter was on its way, and the winds were increasingly chill and rainy. I needed to close the window. But to do so would disrupt my friend's web, perhaps sending it scurrying away forever. No, that was unthinkable. I shivered in the cold, but it was worth it to have the courageous spider with me.

Then came the unforgettable morning:

The overhead light that stayed on all night went off, and I awoke for the few precious minutes of darkness before the sun rose. With the first rays of light entering the cell, I looked up at the spider's web. It was gone! And so was the spider.

During the night the wind had torn the web apart. Only a few filmy shreds trembled in the air. I panicked. Where was my friend? My eyes scanned from corner to corner, from wall to wall.

Minutes passed. A gust of chilling wind blew through the window. I sat motionless, overcome by sadness. I had come to look upon the spider as a messenger of hope, a God-sent creature. Now every hope had been torn from me. This was the darkest moment I'd known.

Out of the corner of my eye I saw something move. Was it the wind blowing something?

I looked up. In a corner of the ceiling was the spider.

For the first time in months I smiled. Not only was my friend there, but it was back at work, determinedly spinning its fragile cables, creating a new web.

Now I knew it was true. God had sent that spider to me. Don't give up, He was saying to me. He had not left me alone in my prison cell. God was there.

In the days that followed, the spider moved from place to place and rebuilt its web throughout the cell. Once I crouched and followed as it moved across the floor, finally settling in a crevice of the wall, where it wove a thick web that enclosed its body like a cocoon. And then one day I watched as the spider went beneath my bed and never emerged. But by now I knew that whatever fate befell it – and me – we were both creatures of God and part of something more vast than we could imagine.

I remained in No.1 Detention House for six-and-a-half years – years filled with deprivation, sickness and, at times, torture. When I was finally released in 1973, I learned that my daughter had been beaten to death during an interrogation by the Red Guards. If I had not been a Christian, I would not have wanted to live. But I knew that my Lord expected me to carry on.

Today I am alive and well. My old life was torn from me, but like the spider, I have learned to build a new one. And it is beautiful.

SILENCE IN THE SNOW

by Steve Smart

On Christmas Eve, 1981, a small, six-seater Cherokee plane carrying five people crashed onto a remote ridge high in one of the most rugged ranges of Colorado's Rocky Mountains. Gary Meeks, a construction executive, was piloting the plane that carried his wife, Pat, his two sons (Arnie, eighteen, and Darren, fifteen) and friend and former business associate, Steve Smart, thirty-four. They were on their way to a skiing vacation when the plane seemed to lose power. All five survived the subsequent crash-landing, but with Pat seriously hurt and Steve unconscious, Gary left the plane to search for help. More than twenty-four hours later Steve slowly regained consciousness. Here is Steve's story of what followed.

Friday, Christmas Day: It took all afternoon today to clear my head. I was so groggy – every time I looked out the window of our wrecked plane at the mountainous granite walls, rocky outcroppings and towering jack pines, all half-hidden behind a veil of blowing snow, I'd think it was just a bad dream. But then I'd look around at Pat and the boys, their faces filled with fear and concern, shivering in the frosty cabin, and I'd realise again what had happened. But I don't remember the crash at all. All I know now is that my shoulder is separated and it's cold and cramped and I'm in pain.

But Pat's the most seriously hurt. 'I think my back may be broken,' she told me. The boys seem fine; they told me they went out yesterday to pack snow around a back cargo door that had sprung open. With the suitcases piled in front of the door, it's a pretty good seal. It'll keep some of the cold out. Against all odds, and because of Gary's skill when he belly flopped the plane into a snowbank, we have a pretty good capsule to survive in. For awhile. There's no food; Christmas dinner tonight was a handful of snow. We're wearing only street clothes and light coats. Most of our ski clothes and equipment were shipped ahead. Only the boys have winter parkas and boots.

I wonder if anybody else knows we've crashed? No matter. There's nothing for us to do but wait for somebody to find us – a white plane half-buried in snow.

Saturday: Last night was horrible! It came quickly and lingered long, fifteen hours of the most overpowering blackness I've ever experienced. Every ten minutes I was looking at my watch, wondering when, if ever, the night would be over. Up here, the wind shrieks through the trees, a sound almost too painful to listen to. And it's cold – oh, so very cold. We slept only in fitful bursts. The rest of the time, we talked a little, and prayed, for Gary. We prayed that he made it through safely. But did he? Then we just stared – into the heart of darkness.

It's snowing and blowing even harder and more furiously than yesterday. Arnie and Darren did venture out of the plane to look for Gary, but found nothing. Once I heard a distinct crack and whirled around in my seat, only to see a branch had snapped off a nearby tree. The boys tried to use the wood to start a signal fire, but the wind kept blowing it out.

But what a moment today! Arnie was cleaning out his suitcase – he was going to fill it with snow for eating – when he found his Bible. I've never been that thrilled about a Bible before. But we all took turns reading favourite passages.

Our spirits are much higher tonight than this morning. I was even kidding the boys about our 'gourmet' diet.

'What'll it be tonight?' I'd asked them.

'A pizza with pepperoni and peppers,' ordered Arnie.

'Double cheeseburger, large order of fries, and a chocolate shake,' Darren said.

And I reached out of the little window near me and grabbed a glob of snow. 'Lets see now,' I said, holding out a snowball. 'Which one of you gets the pizza?'

I've taken off my watch – looking at it makes the days last too long.

Sunday: As tired as I was last night, sleep still came only sporadically. Once I awoke with a start – I couldn't feel my body. It was numb all over. I panicked. Frantically I rubbed myself, until the feeling finally came back. But when the feeling came back, so did the pain, especially in my shoulder. Finally, gritting my teeth, I yanked on the shoulder and, to my amazement, it popped back into place!

This morning I heard two planes fly overhead, but we couldn't see them; it's still snowing as fiercely as ever. Little things inside the plane tell me our time is slowly running out. I can feel it in the numbness of my feet. And the boys are becoming quieter. We don't joke about the snow anymore – in fact, we don't even eat it. Arnie discovered that the hoarfrost growing thicker and thicker on the inside walls of the cabin tastes better than snow. We use credit cards to scrape it off. We keep the window clear that way, too – we need that lifeline to the world.

Mostly, though, we just huddled close today. Arnie brought out his Bible and we read. How much like the psalmist we feel, crying out to God in the midst of our despair.

The boys, with their long but neatly kept brown hair, flashing dark eyes and endless energy, remind me of Gary. If I dwell too much on him or friends or our situation, it becomes too much to bear, and I just have to weep, my whole body heaving with deep, wrenching sobs. It happens to all of us. Our remedy is to hug each other, as tightly as we can. That simple touch seems to supply as much strength as it does warmth to a shivering body. It's so cold, and hope is so hard to find.

Monday: I heard it shortly after daylight – a low throbbing sound in the distance. It was coming closer, its rhythmic thub-thub-thub unmistakable. A helicopter! Darren saw it first. As it got closer to us it slowed, and then began descending to the bottom of the valley about a half-mile from the plane.

'They're landing! They've found us!' one of the boys shouted. How can I describe the joy that pulsed through each of us as we watched seven, eight, nine people jump out of the big, olive-green chopper and begin snowshoeing their way through the trees toward us. We were all hugging each other and thanking God, hollering and singing and carrying on in the best tradition.

The big chopper flew off again as we excitedly squirmed in our cramped seats, waiting for the people to work their way up to us. We couldn't go out to meet them – chest-deep snow and frozen feet precluded that. 'It sure is taking them a long time,' Pat said. 'Can we signal to them somehow?' We yelled but the wind was still too loud.

'It's getting dark,' Darren said, and almost immediately the helicopter reappeared, coming over the mountain as I had heard that morning, settling down in the same spot in the same little valley kicking up the same snow. We watched with wide eyes as our rescue party began to reboard the chopper. We saw it all! Our desperate screams reached only our own ears. The helicopter lifted off disappeared into the dusk. They hadn't seen us – they didn't even know we were here!

How can I explain the devastation we all felt? All we had been holding out for, hoping for, had been cruelly snatched away. We all broke into tears and sobbed. But finally, after about an hour, when the tears had stopped, Arnie pulled out his Bible and we read some more. How real the words of Psalm 22 became to us. 'My God why have you abandoned me? I have cried desperately for help, but still it does not come.... Our ancestors put their trust in you, they trusted you, and you saved them.' We must continue to trust, to wait for our rescue.

Monday night: It's been the best and worst night of my entire life. All night long the wind has moaned eerily. None of us can sleep, at least not for long, and somebody has to be awake at all times to make sure Darren stays awake. His body temperature has dropped so dramatically that we're afraid we might lose him if we let him sleep. So we've been talking most of the time – sometimes praying, sometimes sharing the private concerns of our hearts. Tonight, we all prayed that God would do with us what he wanted. We've put our lives entirely in His hands now.

What a turning point that has been for me! Before the crash, I'd got to the point in my life where I'd quit praying. I didn't feel worthy or faithful enough to God to even approach Him, when so often I'd ignored Him. I hated to reach out to God because that made me examine myself, and that hurt. But these last days I've known His presence. How alive those old Bible stories have become. I'm the prodigal son of the parable, flawed, coming on my knees to ask for the barest essentials. I want that relationship with my Father again.

We talked a lot about faith tonight – what was our purpose here, why were there so many obstacles in life?

'Steve, what have you found?' Arnie asked me. 'How do you get through hard times? And why, why are they there?'

'I don't know why we have them – they sure keep coming, don't they?' I said. 'But I do know this. It seems that every time I've lived through a tough time, and stopped to look, I've learned something. Something good.'

'What good has come from this, Steve?'

I marvel at the resilience of Arnie's spirit. His questions come from deep within, with no tinge of bitterness. He knows we're all slowly freezing to death, yet like the psalmist he's still grasping for that hope. I want so badly to give him that, to give him life. But that's not mine to do. 'Arnie, I don't know what this means for you,' I told him. 'But tonight, when we prayed about putting our lives in God's hands, I experienced a peace I've never felt before. I discovered, for sure, that God will sustain me, no matter what. And that's good.'

The warmth that had grown among us tonight has defied the bitter cold. As we talked, we opened up to one another in a way that affirmed the growing trust we were feeling, not only in God, but in each other. There were tears again, for a father and husband and friend we all know has been gone too long. For relationships, for friendships. But mostly they are tears of joy, for the blessings of God we are only now beginning to fully comprehend.

The moaning wind has stopped. An early morning peace has come to the mountains – and to us.

Tuesday: We were greeted this morning with streaks of sunlight, the first time since the crash. But there was no other sign of life, save two squirrels. It was quiet, peaceful and very cold.

Pat was the first to repeat the question of last night. 'Steve, why are we suffering like this? Why so much?' Her back is really hurting her and, as with the rest of us, the cold has taken a severe toll.

I didn't know what to say. 'Maybe Job will help.' I finally answered. 'Maybe now we can really understand what he has to say about suffering.'

So while Pat's been reading, chapter after chapter, the rest of us have just stared out the window or made small talk. Last night really left us drained.

Pat just closed the Bible – I guess that means she's finished. It's a good thing, too – already the sun has begun to slip down behind the high peaks. I wonder what she found, what she'll say about …

Wait! There's something coming down the hill. It's … it's a person, a man! Where did he come from? I didn't hear anything – no plane, no helicopter. Does he see us? Yes, yes, he does! He's waving and shouting, 'Over here, over here!' There are more of them, two, three, four. They're running down the slope, from over the ridge. Oh, God, thank you, God. You never forgot us, God, in five days here you never left us. You never did – and I know now you never will!

A man's head poked through the door of the cabin.

'Hi, folks,' the man said, shaking the fluffy white coat of powder off his parka. 'It's good to see you!'

The search for Steve, Pat, Arnie and Darren – one of the largest in Colorado history – had only resumed that Tuesday because of the sunshine. The previous night, it was decided that rescuers would make one last-ditch effort to find the plane only if weather permitted. And when Ken Zafren, a medical student from Oregon who had volunteered to be a part of the search party found the four, there was less than an hour of daylight left. The rescuers were shocked to find the four alive. Convinced that the group would be dead, the rescuers wept with joy, along with the survivors, at finding them.

Pat and the two boys were taken off the mountain that night in a helicopter, after the chopper pilot defied darkness and a new blizzard to land his craft on a wobbly boulder near the crash site. Near white-out conditions finally forced him to take off before Steve and some rescuers could be loaded aboard. The next day, in a snowstorm, sixty people helped bring Steve down by sled – it took nine-and-a-half hours.

But this story of faith rediscovered and renewed doesn't end at the base of a mountain – it goes on, like faith itself, growing and developing, encouraging and sustaining. And if anyone ever needed a life-giving faith to endure, those four did.

Steve turned out to be the most seriously hurt; he had both legs amputated below the knee because of frostbite. Pat required back surgery for a fractured vertebra and both boys lost toes, also because of frostbite. For each, it was a long and difficult recovery made more so because of the loss of Gary. His body was finally found in September; after an intensive search. Yet, the courage that faith gives, the knowledge that God was with them, remained alive and vital, and brought healing of both body and spirit.

Today that faith lives stronger, deeper and more vibrant than ever in Steve and Pat and Arnie and Darren. 'The crash was a new beginning for me,' Steve says. 'All that I went through was a small price to pay – for faith.'

USEFUL ADDRESSES

Reading these stories may encourage you to think about your own struggles. If you would like further help on your life journey, here is a list of agencies that may be able to help:

British Association for Counselling
1 Regent Place
Rugby
Warks CV21 2PJ
01788-550899

Families Anonymous (Advice on family problems and drug abuse)
Unit 37
Dodington & Rollo Community Association
Charlotte Despard Avenue
London SW11 5JE
020-7498-4680

ACET (AIDS Advisers)
Central Office
PO Box 3693
London SE15 2BS
020-8780-0400

AGE Concern
Astral House
1268 London Road
London SW16 4ER
020-8679-8000

CRUSE Bereavement care
Cruse House
126 Sheen Road
Richmond
Surrey TW9 1UR
020-8940-4818
MIND (Advice on Mental Health)
020-8522-1728
0345-660-163

Relate (Marriage & Relationship Advice)
Herbert Gray College
Little Church Street
Rugby
CV21 3AP
01788-573-241

*The Institute of Family Therapy (Therapeutic work
with families and couples)*
24–32 Stephenson Way
Euston
London NW1 2HX
020-7391-9150

The Samaritans (General Help-line)
0345-909-090
jo@samaritans.org

Survivors of Sexual Abuse
020-7890-4732